The Brontë Family

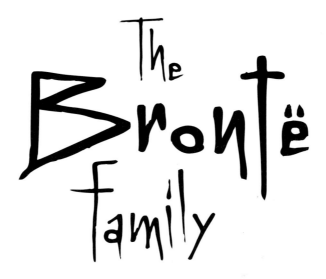

The Brontë Family

passionate literary geniuses

Karen Smith Kenyon

Lerner Publications Company / Minneapolis

To Richard and Yvonne, and to the memory of my parents,
who gave me love of words and music

Lerner Publications Company
A division of Lerner Publishing Group
241 First Avenue North
Minneapolis, MN 55401 U.S.A.

Website address: www.lernerbooks.com

Library of Congress Cataloging-in-Publication Data

Kenyon, Karen Smith.
    The Brontë family : passionate literary geniuses / by Karen Smith Kenyon.
        p.   cm. — (Lerner biographies)
    Includes bibliographical references and index.
    Summary: A joint biography of Charlotte, Emily, Branwell, and Anne Brontë, exploring how the siblings sparked creativity in each other and how their lives were woven into their novels.
    ISBN 0-8225-0071-X (lib. bdg. : alk. paper)
    1. Brontë family—Juvenile literature. 2. Authors, English—19th century—Family relationships—Juvenile literature. 3. Authors, English—19th century—Biography—Juvenile literature. 4. Brontë, Patrick Branwell, 1817–1848—Juvenile literature. 5. Brontë, Charlotte, 1816–1855—Juvenile literature. 6. Brontë, Emily, 1818–1848—Juvenile literature. 7. Brontë, Anne, 1820–1849—Juvenile literature. [1. Brontë family. 2. Authors, English. 3. Brontë, Patrick Branwell, 1817–1848. 4. Brontë, Charlotte, 1816–1855. 5. Brontë, Emily, 1818–1848. 6. Brontë, Anne, 1820–1849.] I. Title. II. Series.
    PR4168 .K46 2003
    823'.809—dc21   2001004957

Manufactured in the United States of America
1 2 3 4 5 6 – JR – 08 07 06 05 04 03

Contents

Whatever now becomes of the work—the occupation of writing it has
been a real boon to me—it took me out of dark and desolate reality to an
unreal but happier region . . . imagination lifted me when I was sinking . . .
I am thankful to God who gave me this faculty.

—*Charlotte Brontë*
to William S. Williams, 29 August 1849

Author's Note

I first visited Haworth, England, and the Brontë Parsonage in 1992. It was pouring rain, and visitors patiently waited with bright umbrellas in the small front garden of the dark stone parsonage—the churchyard behind them, the green undulating moors just beyond. It was August, a weekend, but still I hadn't expected the crowd.

I also didn't expect the way this personal view of the lives of Charlotte, Emily, Anne, and Branwell Brontë and the landscape of Haworth would affect me. We had taken three trains from London to arrive at Haworth—the last a steam train. After the steam train and the walk up the steep cobblestone street, I felt I was in the nineteenth-century world of the Brontës—the sky of billowing dark clouds, the dramatic, wild, green landscape of the moors, the angles of the hills rising in all directions—the woolen shop, the inns, and the church on the site where their father's church once stood.

We all soon found refuge from the rain inside the Parsonage, and it almost felt as if the Brontës were all inside too—or maybe they were waiting patiently for the crowds to disperse and go home so that they could inhabit their home once more. We saw the dining room where Emily, Charlotte, and Anne wrote their novels and poems, now graced with a copy of the famous Richmond portrait of Charlotte. In that same room was the couch where Emily died. We saw the kitchen where Emily baked bread and studied German with a book propped next to her mixing bowl; and the Reverend Brontë's study, where it seemed he might come in any moment to read his newspaper or the Book of Psalms with his magnifying glass. Upstairs we saw Charlotte's lavender beige silk honeymoon dress, many oil portraits by Branwell, and sketches and other paintings by all four siblings, along with a few of the tiny books the children wrote.

When I left and returned to the United States, the Brontës didn't leave me. I could picture them so well—as children creating their magical worlds—Branwell and Charlotte leading the way. And later as they tried to find their work in the world, and even later when their novels poured from them. It was as if they were urging me to read more about them, to learn the details of their lives.

Their story began to take on an almost mythic quality for me, the three sisters as heroines. Reading about their lives, I couldn't help but wish them well through their struggles and sufferings and cheer them on when they persisted and created. And Branwell, too, though his life took on an even more tragic quality, played an important role.

In that clammy, bleak stone parsonage, they didn't have the material goods available today, and so they created their own world of imagination and play. In this biography, I've tried to show how the siblings sparked creativity in each other, and how their lives were woven into their novels.

The Brontës' lives were over too soon. They all died young. But in a sense they are not gone. Their novels—*Jane Eyre, Wuthering Heights, Agnes Grey, The Tenant of Wildfell Hall, Villette, The Professor, Shirley*—and their poetry will always be read, and for those who know their story, or who visit their home, their spirits seem strong and clear.

Two years later, I again visited the Parsonage and the landscape that is so much a part of the Brontës' lives and novels. In a way, it felt like coming home or visiting friends I felt very close to. The presences of these amazing writers are strong there, as others have attested.

A black-and-white cat sat in front of the steps to the front door, as if waiting for them. And, in some ways, I don't doubt that he truly was. It's easy to expect to see them all come rambling home once more across their beloved moors.

Karen Smith Kenyon

9

A street scene in London, about the time Charlotte and Anne Brontë first visited their publisher there

ONE

Setting the Record Straight

We had only confessed ourselves to our publisher. . . . to all the rest of the world we must remain 'gentlemen' as heretofore.

—Charlotte Brontë
to Mary Taylor, 4 September 1848

Charlotte and Anne Brontë made their way along the cobbled streets of 1848 London. They had come to the big city from the Yorkshire village of Haworth in the north of England to set a record straight.

Charlotte, under the pen name of Currer Bell, had written the popular, romantic *Jane Eyre,* the story of a governess in love with her employer. As Acton Bell, the younger Anne had written two novels, *Agnes Grey,* also about a governess, and *The Tenant of Wildfell Hall,* a revealing portrait of alcoholism. Their sister Emily, as Ellis Bell, had written *Wuthering Heights,* the dramatic love story of Catherine and Heathcliff. As she often did, Emily chose to stay at home in the parsonage with the wild moors in her backyard.

Charlotte and Anne were determined to correct the false information that T. C. Newby, the unscrupulous publisher of

Anne's and Emily's books, was spreading—that all of the novels were written by one person—the well-known and popular Currer Bell. Newby had already sold the first sheets of *The Tenant of Wildfell Hall* to an American publisher as the latest work of Currer Bell, the author of *Jane Eyre*. He had affirmed his belief that *Jane Eyre, Wuthering Heights, Agnes Grey,* and *The Tenant of Wildfell Hall* were all the product of this one writer.

Though Emily would have no part of it, Charlotte and Anne decided to go to London to see Charlotte's publisher, Smith, Elder. After taking the night train to London, they stood, tired and timid in their homemade dresses, at 65 Cornhill, a large bookseller's shop in London and home of the offices of the publisher of *Jane Eyre*. The thirty-two-year-old Charlotte, plain and old-fashioned looking, peered up through her spectacles at the handsome young man who introduced himself as George Smith. Charlotte quietly handed him—he was her publisher, after all—a recent letter he had written her, addressed to Currer Bell.

Stunned, his dark eyes looked at her, then back at the letter. "Where did you get this?" he asked.

"From the post office," she said. "It was addressed to me." Then she blurted out, "We are three sisters."

Charlotte later wrote about the meeting: "I laughed at his queer perplexity—a recognition took place—I gave my real name—'Miss Brontë'—we were both hurried from the shop into a little back room—ceiled with a great skylight and only large enough to hold 3 chairs and a desk—and there explanations were rapidly gone into."

Smith quickly made plans to introduce the famous authors to his sisters and mother, and he invited them to the opera. That evening the white-gloved Smith, his mother, and two elegantly clad sisters took Charlotte and Anne to Rossini's *Barber of Seville* at the Opera House. As Charlotte climbed the crimson-carpeted grand staircase in her country garment, she was overcome by the splendor of the surroundings. She later wrote: "They must have thought us queer, quizzical-looking beings, especially me with my spectacles. . . . Fine ladies & gentlemen glanced at us with a slight, graceful superciliousness quite warranted by the circumstances—Still I felt pleasurably excited."

The next day, Smith, with his portly mother, picked up both Brontës in his carriage and took them to dinner. Charlotte felt ridiculous, but she also had the satisfaction of knowing that all the fine ladies and gentlemen who had looked down on her and her sister would have fallen over themselves to meet the author of *Jane Eyre*.

Patrick Brontë, father of five daughters and one son, was a great storyteller at home and in the pulpit of Haworth Church.

TWO

Storyteller

All the girls used to sit in breathless silence, . . . when their father unfolded lurid scene after lurid scene; but the greatest effect was produced on Emily who seemed to be unconscious of everything else except her father's story, and sometimes the descriptions became so vivid, intense and terrible that they had to implore him to desist.

—Cathel O'Byrne,
The Gaelic Source of the Brontë Genius

Maria, Elizabeth, Charlotte, Emily, Anne, and Branwell Brontë sat spellbound. Their large eyes, focused on their father, were full of excitement, fear, and curiosity. The Reverend Patrick Brontë, his Irish brogue soft and fiery by turns, often told his five little girls and only son stories of his father's life in Ireland.

The Brontë children began most days enchanted by their father's stories. Afterward they scurried off to play on the moors, clambering up the path to the inviting slopes. There

were dark blue bilberries to pick from the bushes, blue hare-
bells and pinkish purple heather to gather, and stones to skip
in the stream.

Two years earlier, in April 1820, the family had moved to
the village of Haworth, where the Reverend Brontë took over
duties as minister of the village church. With their six children,
Mr. Brontë and his wife, the petite, elegant Maria, had jour-
neyed all day in a covered wagon to the wild-looking country.

At the top of the cobblestone main road they saw their
new home—a two-storied dark-stone Georgian house. It was
surrounded on three sides by the churchyard full of tall gravestones. But they had a small garden in front—and in back,
beyond the cemetery, lay the rolling free land of the moors
with its grasses, black rocks, and purple heather.

*A churchyard, with its gravestones, surrounded the Brontë
family's new home.*

Maria Brontë, mother of Maria, Elizabeth, Charlotte, Emily, Anne, and Branwell, became ill soon after moving to Haworth.

Soon after moving in, the elder Maria became ill. Before long she lay suffering in a darkened room. The children had to tiptoe around the house and talk in whispers, while their distraught father nursed his wife through the lonely, painful nights. His sister-in-law, Elizabeth Branwell, came north from fashionable Penzance to help out.

Maria Brontë died seven and one-half months later, probably of uterine cancer, repeating over and over, "Oh God my poor children. Oh God my poor children." The oldest, Maria, was seven. Anne was not quite two.

Aunt Branwell stayed on to care for her nieces and nephew. She didn't seem to mind overseeing the upkeep of the house and cooking, as well as teaching her nieces sewing, simple ABCs, and arithmetic. She felt it was her duty to help out.

Every night the Brontë children climbed these stairs to bed.

After supper each night, Maria, Elizabeth, Charlotte, Emily, Anne, and Branwell climbed the stairs to their beds. The rooms were always cold, the flagstone floors bare, and the windows curtainless. Their father feared a fire, so he would allow no curtains or drapes.

The children's enthusiasm for life overcame the cold surroundings. They had each other for comfort and fun. The younger children looked forward to having Maria tell them the news of the day, which her father had discussed with her earlier. Maria relayed the events to her siblings with such drama that they were as good as fairy tales—full of heroes and villains and intrigue. The children were comforted by her stories and by the way she gathered them all together, like a little mother.

Each evening Aunt Branwell came clanking up the stairs in her pattens, the metal clogs villagers often wore outside clamped onto their shoes to keep from sinking in the mud. Aunt Branwell wore them indoors as well, for fear of catching a cold if she walked on the bare stone floor.

And each night, their father would wind the grandfather clock on the stairwell before going upstairs to his room. The candles and oil lamps would all be safely put out, and the two buckets of water, in case of a fire, were put in their place as usual.

Aunt Branwell kept the youngest, Anne, in her room, while Branwell slept in the Reverend Brontë's room, since he was the only boy. Maria, Elizabeth, Charlotte, and Emily snuggled down in their small cots in a tiny room with a view of the churchyard and the moors beyond.

Patrick Brontë's childhood home in Ireland

THREE

Cowan Bridge

And wildly did I cling to thee.
I could not, would not, dared not part
Lest hell again should seize my heart . . .
But we are sundered—thee, thy grave,
And me, this dreary wild will have."

> —Branwell Brontë,
> from "Misery"

A typical day for the Brontë children began with a jolt—the sound of a pistol firing. Each morning their father fired one shot from the gun he kept by his bed at night for protection. He had kept it there since 1811, when he had lived in the neighboring village of Hartshead in the midst of riots at nearby woolen mills.

The Reverend Brontë had come from a poor Irish village, but he had received an excellent education at Cambridge University in England. Because of this, he was able to undertake Branwell's education in the classics, history, geography, and mathematics. He was concerned, however, about his daughters. Education for girls consisted of reading, writing, simple

21

arithmetic, sewing, needlepoint, embroidery, knitting, and "accomplishments," such as French, drawing, and music. It was especially important to educate his daughters, he felt, since their chances for marriage were slim. Brides at this time were expected to bring property or money to a marriage, and he knew that with his poor salary he would never be able to afford to give them this.

Then he had heard of the Clergy Daughters' School at Cowan Bridge in Lancashire, about fifty miles from Haworth. Here the daughters of needy churchmen could be educated. The school was run by a prominent and wealthy clergyman, the Reverend William Carus Wilson. The Reverend Wilson, however, believed that females were weak and sinful, and he ran his school in a way meant to keep them humble. The well-meaning Reverend Brontë was unaware of Wilson's attitudes,

The Clergy Daughters' School at Cowan Bridge

and the pamphlets for the school promised just the education he felt his daughters needed.

During the late winter and the spring of 1824, whooping cough, measles, and chicken pox passed through Haworth and the parsonage. All six Brontë children came down with whooping cough and were put to their beds. But by July, Maria and Elizabeth were sufficiently recovered to go to the Cowan Bridge school. Charlotte and Emily were scheduled to join them soon.

When the Reverend Brontë accompanied Maria and Elizabeth to the school, he spent the night and toured the buildings, which appeared to meet his standards. He had no qualms about leaving his two daughters.

But Cowan Bridge proved to be dismal and unhealthy. The morning's oatmeal porridge was often burned, and the midday beef was spoiled. An odor of rancid fat steamed from the oven in which most of the food was prepared. The rain-water used to make the rice pudding was full of the dust it collected from the roof. Maria and Elizabeth were used to simple food, prepared with cleanliness and care. Still not strong because of their bouts of sickness, they began to go without eating.

In August Mr. Brontë took Charlotte to Cowan Bridge, and by November 1824, Emily seemed healthy enough to join her sisters. When Mr. Brontë escorted her to Cowan Bridge, the older girls must not have complained to him about the harsh circumstances of the school, and he returned home unaware of the tragedy that was brewing.

Each Sunday all the students of Cowan Bridge had to walk two miles to Tunstall Church to hear the Reverend Wilson preach. In winter Maria, Elizabeth, Charlotte, and Emily made the walk shivering and half-starved. The cold did not

Maria and Elizabeth were buried in the Haworth Church next to their mother.

cease inside the church, as dampness clung to the walls and crept in the windows.

In the spring, Maria grew ill. She coughed, lost weight, grew feverish, and rapidly grew worse. Many people in the eighteenth and nineteenth centuries died of tuberculosis, and since Maria had the symptoms of this dreaded contagious disease, Mr. Brontë was informed and sent for her immediately. When he saw Maria, he was shocked at the sight of his thin, pale child.

At the parsonage, Maria, too weak and limp even to speak, was placed in the sickroom upstairs, just as her mother had been. Maria died of tuberculosis on May 6, 1825, at age eleven. The Reverend Brontë was again devastated, and all the children, but especially Branwell, were overcome with sorrow.

At Cowan Bridge, the school staff now looked with anxiety on Elizabeth, who had developed symptoms similar to Maria's. Soon she was sent home too. The very next day, Mr. Brontë removed Charlotte and Emily from the school as well. Elizabeth, ten, died at the parsonage just two weeks later, on June 15.

The countryside was coming to life. Lilacs bloomed lavender and white in the parsonage garden, but now both Maria and Elizabeth were buried alongside their mother under the church floor.

Three of the little books written by the Brontë children

four

The Twelve Soldiers

*Out of barren desert arose a palace of diamond,
the pillar of which were ruby and emerald
illuminated with lamps too bright to look upon.
The Genius led us into a hall of sapphire in
which were thrones of gold. On the thrones sat
the Princes of the Genii. In the midst of the hall
hung a lamp like a sun. Around it stood genii
and fairies without whose robes were of beaten
gold sparkling with diamonds.*

—Charlotte Brontë,
from *The Early Writings of Charlotte Brontë*

Charlotte was nine, Branwell eight, Emily seven, and
Anne five the autumn when Tabitha Akroyd, a fifty-three-year-
old Yorkshire woman, came to live as a servant at the parsonage. She was shrewd, practical, and loving.

The motherly Tabby came with a sense of the moors and
countryside—its history, folklore, and scandals. Charlotte,
Branwell, Emily, and Anne would gather in the kitchen while
Tabby cooked and baked, the steam and scent of potatoes,

27

turnips, pudding, and cakes filling the small room. Then, with a far-off look in her eyes, Tabby would begin to tell stories of the early days in the area, how the packhorses went through once a week with their tinkling bells, or about the valley where she believed fairies appeared on moonlit nights.

Though the children were at home and not in school, they still were busy with lessons, and the parsonage settled into a routine. Aunt Branwell instructed the girls at regular hours in sewing, while their father taught Branwell Latin, Greek, geography, and history and also instructed his daughters less intensely. When the three daily papers arrived, all the children gathered around their father to learn about England's world expansion. It was a time of industrial development as well—the steam train alone was changing people's lives. In the afternoons, the family engaged in discussions of the week's political events, new poetry, and articles in literary magazines. Still, much of the children's time was either spent streaking across the moors or telling stories to each other in the upstairs study.

Then, on June 5, 1826, an event occurred that swept them into a fantasy world that would continue all their lives. Their father, after a trip to nearby Leeds, came home with twelve new wooden soldiers for Branwell. He also brought a bowling game for Charlotte, a toy village for Emily, and a dancing doll for Anne. But it was Branwell's soldiers that engaged their imaginations. Charlotte wrote:

> Branwell came to our door with a box of soldiers Emily & I jumped out of bed and I snat[c]hed up one & exclaimed this is the Duke of Wellington it shall be mine!! [Wellington was the current prime minister of England, and he had defeated the French leader Napoléon Bonaparte at the famous Battle of Waterloo.]

> When I said this Emily likewise took one & said it should be hers when Anne came down she took one also. Mine was the prettiest of the whole & perfect in every part Emilys was a Grave looking fellow we called him Gravey. Anne's was a queer little thing very much like herself. [H]e was called Waiting Boy[.] Branwell chose Bonaparte.

From the moment the wooden figures came into their lives, they seemed to be more than toys and took on lives of their own. The characters were more real to the children than the inhabitants of their father's parish. The soldiers were moved about like puppets—sometimes put in the garden or in the cellar or taken to the moors, or the children would become the characters themselves and act out the parts.

The early stories and plays featuring the soldiers developed into an ongoing African adventure where the fearless soldiers of the sagas went on dangerous missions to the northwest coast of Africa and founded what their authors called Glass Town, a mixture of London, Paris, and Babylon.

Each child's soldier had his own colony in this new land. They called themselves the four Genii, the name inspired by *The Arabian Nights.* The idea of the Genii was that the children could preside over their imaginary worlds and still weave themselves into the stories. The four became completely involved in the games and only stopped for meals and lessons. At times Tabby was concerned about their intensity and passion.

By 1829 Charlotte and Branwell had written down eighteen of their stories. In addition, Branwell decided the Young Men should have their own version of *Blackwood's Magazine,* a favorite family publication full of satire, politics, religion, and the arts. The children's literary creations were very tiny—the books were sometimes written on used sugar bags and ranged in size from 1 ½ x 2 ½ inches to later ones of 6 ½ x 7 inches. The writing in them was so small it is almost indecipherable. Perhaps the children enjoyed the extra secrecy this provided.

For eight more years, Charlotte and Branwell wrote their Glass Town sagas, which later concentrated on the imaginary and exotic kingdom they called Angria. Writing became a power game for the two siblings as they tried to outmaneuver each other in character and plot.

After a while, Emily and Anne decided to begin their own kingdom and pulled away from their involvement with the Angrian stories. They created Gondal, a rough and wild land with plain simple folk, dominated by a woman, Augusta Geraldine Almeda. Unfortunately, little survives of Emily's and Anne's parts of all these stories.

Replicas of three soldiers frame one of the tiny books written by the Brontë children.

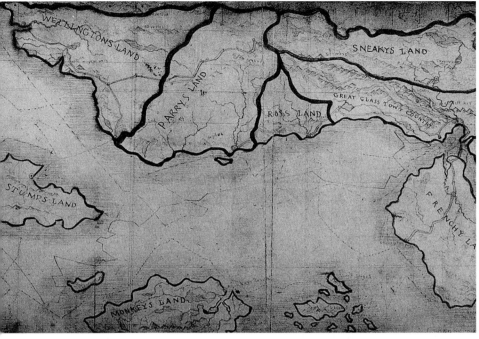

Branwell's map of Angria and Glass Town

By the time Charlotte was fourteen, she had written twenty-two volumes, and Branwell had equaled her output. Mr. Brontë arranged art lessons for his children and took Charlotte and Branwell to visit the studio of a well-known artist and architect who lived nearby. All of the children made watercolors and drawings to illustrate the stories and lands they created. Emily added her dogs, Grasper, and later Keeper, and her hawk, Hero, as subjects for her art. The whitewashed walls of Charlotte and Emily's room were decorated with pencil sketches of faces, animals, and flowers.

The epic tales grew as the children inspired each other. Their creativity and writing ability were developing as they worked alone and together.

Charlotte was first a student, then a teacher at Roe Head School.

FIVE

Roe Head

Must I from day to day sit chained to this chair prisoned within these four bare walls, while these glorious summer suns are burning in heaven and the year is revolving in its richest glow and declaring at the close of every summer day it will never come again?

—Charlotte Brontë,
Roe Head Journal, 11 August 1836

In January 1831, Charlotte, fourteen, was sent to Roe Head School, twenty miles from Haworth. This would be Charlotte's first venture away from home since the tragic experience of Cowan Bridge. There were fewer than twelve girls in the school, most from nearby manufacturing families.

While at Roe Head, Charlotte found the first friends she had outside of her family—Mary Taylor and Ellen Nussey. They remained her friends throughout her life. Mary later wrote of Charlotte's arrival at the school:

> I first saw her coming out of a covered cart, in very
> old-fashioned clothes, and looking very cold and mis-
> erable.... She looked a little, old woman, so short-
> sighted that she always appeared to be seeking
> something, and moving her head from side to side to
> catch sight of it. She was very shy and nervous and
> spoke with a strong Irish accent.

Charlotte's adjustment to Roe Head, run by Miss Margaret Wooler and her four sisters, was difficult and painful.
The other students' clothes, even their accents, were different from hers. She was deeply homesick and dwelled on the
memory of her two dead sisters, Maria and Elizabeth.

Despite Charlotte's extreme shyness, she was determined to learn as much as she could. And though at first her
skills in grammar and geography were below the other students', she soon emerged as head of the class, and even won
three prizes. The friendships Charlotte made enriched her
personal and social life. As she overcame her shyness, she
sometimes told ghost stories at night with such enthusiasm
and realism that her classmates were properly terrified.

Charlotte studied at Roe Head for eighteen months, until
July 1832. Meanwhile, at home, her departure changed the
dynamics considerably. Anne moved from Aunt Branwell's room
for the first time to sleep with Emily in the children's study. It
was then Emily and Anne began their legends of Gondal.

We know a little of the hopes, plans, and state of affairs
in the Gondal sagas from Emily's and Anne's diary writings,
though the stories themselves have not survived. Gondal was
a large island with ruined castles and snow-capped moun-
tains. The stories involved dungeons, civil wars, royal princes
and princesses in exile. It appears to have been a place of
female power.

Branwell painted this family portrait of Charlotte, Anne, Branwell, and Emily.

About this time, the Reverend Brontë decided Branwell, then seventeen, should have a profession. And since Branwell didn't seem interested in going to Cambridge to train for the ministry, his father engaged the painter William Robinson to give his son painting lessons. The plan was for Branwell to follow in Robinson's footsteps to the Royal Academy in London. It was at this time that Branwell began to spend most evenings drinking at the Black Bull Pub not far from the parsonage.

By summer 1832, Charlotte was back home and prepared to share her knowledge with her sisters. For the next three years, Charlotte, Aunt Branwell, and Mr. Brontë all provided instruction. The girls took long walks on the moors and all four siblings continued the sagas of Angria and Gondal. In many ways it was an ideal time for the family.

During this period, in 1834, Branwell, still studying with William Robinson, did his well-known painting of his sisters, referred to as the "pillar portrait." It was originally a family portrait of Branwell and his sisters, but for some reason he removed himself from it by painting over his likeness with an image of a white pillar.

Branwell had painted one other family portrait earlier. In

The pillar portrait of Anne, Emily, and Charlotte, painted by Branwell in 1834. The white streak near the center is where Branwell painted himself out.

All the Brontë siblings learned to play this piano at the parsonage.

that one, they are all gathered around a table on which Branwell has placed his trophies of the day's hunting. Only the profile of Emily remains.

Mr. Brontë bought a cottage piano for the family, and all siblings but Charlotte learned to play. Emily was especially gifted. In Charlotte's case, it seems her shortsightedness made it difficult for her to see the music.

A poem Charlotte wrote in December of 1835 reflects on the creative childhood they all experienced:

> We wove a web in childhood
> A web of sunny air;
> We dug a spring in infancy
> Of water pure and fair;
>
> We sowed in youth a mustard seed
> We cut an almond rod;
> We are now grown up to riper age—
> Are they withered in the sod?
>
> The mustard-seed in distant land
> Bends down a mighty tree,
> The dry unbudding almond wand
> Has torched eternity.

On July 29,1835, Charlotte, then nineteen, returned to Roe Head, this time as a teacher. Emily, seventeen, accompanied her. One of the reasons Charlotte took the position was because it included the offer that she could bring along a sister who would receive free tuition.

Branwell may have hoped to prepare himself for the Royal Academy of Art, but he never concentrated on producing the kind of classical drawings that the Academy would require. He seemed torn between his desires to be an artist and a poet. During this period, he wrote several times to *Blackwood's Magazine,* urging them to read his submissions. But the brash tone of his letters did nothing to help him gain the editor's attention.

So he turned back to the history of Angria, filling page after page with verse, and he devoted every other free moment to sketching, painting, and drawing views of new lands discovered by his heroes. He sent Charlotte bulletins on the latest Angrian developments—and Charlotte, when she found any private time, would dream and write about her own beloved Angrian people.

Meanwhile, Emily could not endure the regulations and lack of privacy at Roe Head. She even had to share her bed with two of her fellow pupils. Having no time alone made it difficult for her to engage in her fantasies of Gondal, so there was nothing to make the rigid routine bearable for this girl who best loved her dreamworld and the moors. She grew pale and gaunt and was so homesick she could not eat. Charlotte was alarmed and later wrote:

> Liberty was the breath of Emily's nostrils; without it she perished. . . . Every morning when she woke, the vision of home and the moors rushed on her, and darkened and saddened the day that lay before her.

So three months after Emily arrived at Roe Head, she was back in Haworth. Before long, Anne, almost sixteen, was sent in her place. It was Anne's first time to leave home to go to school. She was quiet and diligent and made no memorable impression on her teachers or fellow students. She knew she needed to gain an education in order to earn her own living.

With Branwell and Emily both home, Emily became her brother's friend and support as his drinking increased. She helped her aunt and Tabby care for the parsonage, wrote poetry, and worked on her Gondal stories. A dark, brooding male figure began to appear in her writings.

Emily loved to work in the kitchen with Tabby—reading while she helped bake bread. A misfortune befell Tabby,

A sketch of Emily Brontë and her dogs from Emily's diary

however, during Christmas of 1836. When Charlotte and Anne came home for their break, they discovered that Tabby, in her sixties, had fallen on the icy streets and broken her leg. When the three girls were told by Aunt Branwell that Tabby would have to be moved to her sister's house to recover, they went on a hunger strike to protest. At last Tabby was allowed to stay and recuperate in the parsonage household.

When Charlotte returned to Roe Head, she began to think about her desire to write. She sent a letter on December 29, 1836, full of excitement, to the offical poet laureate of England—Robert Southey—asking his advice on her poetry. Southey replied over two months later, in a discouraging letter:

> Literature cannot be the business of a woman's life, and it ought not to be. The more she is engaged in her proper duties, the less leisure she will have for it, even as an accomplishment and recreation.

He expressed the prevailing attitude toward women who wrote. The etiquette books of the day advised that women should only be knowledgeable in the domestic spheres. Charlotte concealed her anger in an apologetic, though sarcastic, response: "Sometimes when I'm teaching or sewing I would rather be reading or writing, but I try to deny myself." Then she continued:

> [A]t first perusal of your letter I felt only shame and regret that I had ever ventured to trouble you with my crude rhapsody; I felt a painful heat rise to my face when I thought of the quires of paper I had covered with what once gave me so much delight, but which now was only a source of confusion. . . . I trust I shall never more feel ambitious to see my name in print; if the wish should rise, I'll look at Southey's letter, and suppress it.

Charlotte wrote sixty poems between January 1837 and July 1838, perhaps in defiance of Southey's words.

Anne remained at Roe Head for two years in all. She continued to be quiet and diligent and even won a medal for good conduct. When she became ill at the school and remained sick throughout the winter, Charlotte was frantic as she remembered Maria and Elizabeth. Eventually, Anne was sent home. Charlotte continued to struggle at Roe Head to contain her imaginary world, but finally she left the confining atmosphere of the school and returned home herself in May of 1838.

Charlotte worked as a governess at Stonegappe, above, where she described the children she cared for as "riotous, perverse, and unmanageable."

Six

Seeking and Searching

No one but myself can tell how hard a governess's work is to me—for no one but myself is aware how utterly averse my whole mind and nature are to the employment. Do not think that I fail to blame myself for this, or that I leave any means unemployed to conquer this feeling.

—Charlotte Brontë
to Ellen Nussey, 3 March 1841

In 1838 Anne was eighteen and Charlotte, the eldest, was twenty-two. It was time to become established in careers. Charlotte, Emily, and Anne realized that positions as governesses and teachers were the only professions open to them—but in truth, they all detested the idea. Though Branwell's future was uncertain, his father and aunt still expected that he would be a great success at something.

Charlotte returned to Roe Head at Miss Wooler's request for a short while. She left for good in the fall of 1838. About that time, Emily began teaching at Law Hill School in Halifax, England, trying once again to fit into the outer world. She did find comfort in her poetry—writing it while her students slept and after her needlepoint was put away. In her poems, she yearned for the moors and spring—and perhaps for Gondal.

Branwell had been in the town of Bradford since June 1838, attempting to be a portrait painter. Though he enjoyed some success with commissions—even painting the vicar of Bradford—he was never more than competent, never the brilliant artist his father had expected. He was also spending more and more time in pubs with his friends, drinking too much. By March 1839, he was home—having run up sizable debts and much the worse from his drinking.

At the beginning of March, Charlotte, who never considered herself attractive, received her first marriage proposal. Henry Nussey, the brother of her good friend, Ellen, asked for her hand. He had decided it was time he married, and so he set out in a cool, efficient way to pursue this goal. But Charlotte, who had a more romantic notion about marriage, declined, stating in a letter to Ellen:

> [T]hough I esteemed Henry—though I had a kindly leaning towards him because he is an amiable—well-disposed man yet I had not, and I never could have that intense attachment which could make me willing to die for him—and if I ever marry, it must be in that light of adoration that I will regard my Husband.

By the end of March or early April, Emily was home as well, having tolerated Law Hill for only six months. She told her pupils she preferred the house dog to any of them. When the founder of the school saw how weak and thin Emily had grown, she sent her back home to the parsonage.

About that time, Anne found a position as governess with the Inghams of Blake Hall in Mirfield. Charlotte worried because Anne had a slight stammer when nervous and feared

Charlotte drew this portrait of Anne.

what Mrs. Ingham might think. But Anne evidently had more serious challenges while with the Inghams, such as her discipline problems with the two Ingham children. On one occasion, Mrs. Ingham walked into the schoolroom to find that Anne had tied the children to a table leg in a desperate attempt to keep them at their lessons.

One month later, Charlotte too was working as a governess for a Mrs. Sidgwick at the Sidgwicks' summer house at Stonegappe, twenty miles north of Haworth. During this time, Charlotte thought over her life and decided it was time to give up her childhood dreams and fantasies of Angria, though she realized she could never give up writing, despite Southey's negative comments.

Charlotte's first experience as a governess was difficult. She wrote letters describing her frustration with the children, whom she described as riotous, perverse, and unmanageable cubs. She wrote to Emily:

> I see now more clearly than I have ever done before that a private governess has no existence, is not considered as a living and rational being except as connected with the wearisome duties she has to fulfil. While she is teaching the children, working for them, amusing them, it is all right. If she steals a moment for herself she is a nuisance.

At home in Haworth, Emily occupied herself baking and caring for the house. She jotted down poems about Gondal and about nature on scraps of paper and studied German and music. She was sure to keep a light in the window for Branwell on nights when he stayed out late drinking with friends at the Black Bull. Branwell was the only Brontë who mingled socially with the villagers, and when he was feeling cheerful he could enliven any gathering.

One of Emily's poems muses on her feelings for Branwell and for all she saw as weak or failed:

> Do I despise the timid deer
> Because his limbs are fleet with fear?
> Or would I mock the wolf's death-howl
> Because his form is gaunt and foul?
> Or hear with joy the leverets cry
> Because it cannot bravely die?
>
> No—then above his memory
> Let pity's heart as tender be;
> Say, Earth lie lightly on that breast
> And, Kind Heaven, grant that spirit rest!

The children's study became Emily's room. She kept her camp bed next to the window for dreaming as she gazed out on the churchyard and the moors beyond, and she had a low chair to sit in while writing.

Keeper, Emily's dog, in a drawing by Emily

Emily had a love of wild things, and her menagerie of creatures was growing during this period. She had her two pet geese, Victoria and Adelaide; the merlin, Hero, a bird that she found wounded on the moors and nursed back to health; and her dog, a great bull-mastiff named Keeper. Keeper was a fiend of a dog that terrified everyone but Emily. She seemed a match for all wild creatures.

By mid-July, Charlotte was again at home. Not long after, she had a second, equally unexpected marriage proposal— this one from an Irish curate, David Pryce. He was witty and charming, and he proposed the day after meeting her, after spending only one day in the parish. Charlotte thought of this only as an amiable and unlikely joke. "Well thought I—I've heard of love at first sight but this beats all."

Once they were both home, Charlotte and Emily could

enjoy their time together—picking currants, having dinner and tea, writing at the dining table at night.

In August there was a happy change at the parsonage. William Weightman, their father's new, twenty-five-year-old curate, arrived. Weightman, with his curly hair and good looks, was flirtatious and clever. He had a warm, generous nature that brought cheer as he visited the poorest of the parish.

By December of 1839, Anne was back home too. She had been dismissed after nine months as governess for the two difficult, oldest Ingham children. William Weightman was winning hearts at the parsonage with his good looks and his sympathy, charm, and sense of humor. Once Anne and the new curate met, according to Charlotte, they seemed to take a special interest in one another. She wrote of this time: "He [Weightman] sits opposite Anne at the Church, sighing softly and looking out of the corners of his eyes to attract her attention; and Anne is so quiet, her looks so downcast, they are a picture."

All three of the sisters liked to pretend they found the young curate absurd, but the truth is they found him irresistible. His thoughtfulness showed when, aware that the sisters had never received valentines, he wrote verses and made a card for each, then walked ten miles to mail them.

Branwell decided to follow his sisters' leads, to try to earn his own way as a tutor. With his sound classical training, he secured a position with a Mr. Postlethwaite as tutor to his two sons. But by midsummer, he was dismissed from this position—probably for neglecting his charges.

Soon Branwell embarked on yet another venture. He took a job as assistant clerk-in-charge on the Manchester–Leeds Railway at Sowerby Bridge near Halifax. The railway was new

A prospective governess is interviewed by the family in this nineteenth-century illustration.

and must have seemed exciting. Branwell leaped at the opportunity to work on it.

By May 1840, despite the fact that her first position as a governess had ended poorly, Anne accepted a job as governess for the Reverend Edmund Robinson and his wife, Lydia, at Thorp Green Hall, near the city of York. Anne, who was gentle and sweet, seemed to have an inner strength that served her well. Of the three sisters, she was the only one able to tolerate being a governess for any length of time. She eventually worked at Thorp Green for five years.

In March 1841, Charlotte tried governessing again—this time for a Mrs. White of Rawdon, who had a girl of eight and a boy of six. According to Charlotte, the children were "wild and unbroken." On the day Charlotte left for her duties at Rawdon, Emily, who cherished her freedom, wrote one of her most famous poems. In it she describes herself as a "chain-less soul."

The Old Stoic

Riches I hold in light esteem;
And Love I laugh to scorn;
And lust of fame was but a dream
That vanished with the morn:

And if I pray, the only prayer
That moves my lips for me
Is, "Leave the heart that now I hear,
And give me liberty!"

Yes, as my swift days near their goal,
'Tis all that I implore;
In life and death, a chainless soul,
With courage to endure.

Meanwhile, Branwell, despite some drinking, seemed to be doing fine. After a year and a month of railway service, he was promoted to a new site and position in the valley of Lud-denden Foot. There Branwell mixed with the townspeople of nearby Luddenden, a center of the textile trade. He attended concerts in Halifax and drew sketches of local manufacturers. And within a month of taking up his post on June 5, 1841, he had a poem, "Heaven and Earth," published in the *Halifax Guardian*. He went to pubs as well, but often for the purpose of meeting with other writers and artists.

In July of 1841, a new idea was brewing at the parsonage. Charlotte and Emily would open their own school. Aunt Branwell had offered them a loan from her savings to begin it, and their father was encouraging. Charlotte decided they first needed more training, especially in languages. She had been receiving letters from Mary Taylor written from Brussels, Belgium, where she was traveling. Charlotte's desire to see for herself the soaring cathedrals and the art of that city made her think of Brussels as a place to receive training.

Still working at Rawdon, she wrote a very diplomatic and convincing letter to their aunt. Charlotte pointed out that she and Emily must acquire an education of "superiority," especially in the form of accomplishments, such as music, drawing, and foreign languages:

> I feel an absolute conviction that, if this advantage were allowed us, it would be the making of us for life. Papa will perhaps think it a wild & ambitious scheme; but who ever rose in the world without ambition? When he left Ireland to go to Cambridge University, he was as ambitious as I am now. I want us all to go on. I know we have talents, and I want them to be turned to account. I look to you, aunt, to help us. I think you will not refuse.

The result was that Aunt Branwell agreed to finance their further education abroad so that they would be better prepared to teach young girls. In December Charlotte resigned from her much-disliked job with the Whites at Rawdon.

Martha Taylor, Mary's sister, was going to school in Brussels, but Martha's school was too expensive for the Brontës. Eventually, the Pensionnat Heger, also in Brussels, was highly recommended by a family friend in that city.

So, at dawn on February 8, 1842, Charlotte and Emily, accompanied by the Reverend Brontë, climbed into a hired gig, as Aunt Branwell, wrapped in a heavy shawl, stood in the parsonage doorway. They were setting off for Brussels and the Pensionnat Heger. But first the horse cart would take them to Leeds, where they would take the train to London, Charlotte's and Emily's first visit to that famous city.

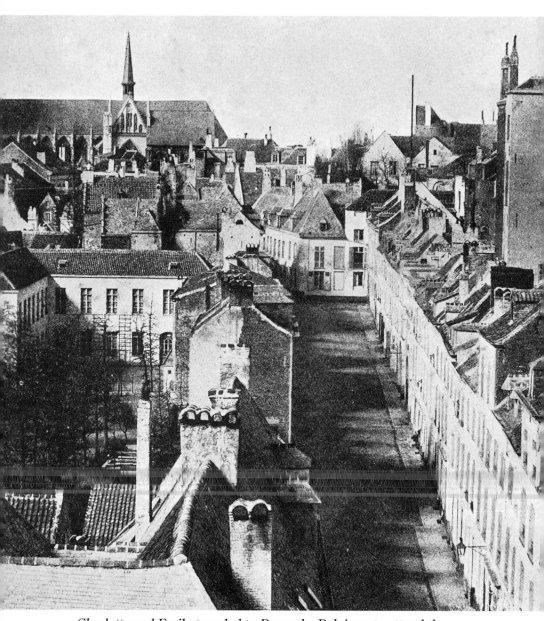

Charlotte and Emily traveled to Brussels, Belgium, to attend the Pensionnat Heger, left foreground.

ȘEVEN

Brussels and After

*I was twenty-six years old a week or two since,
and at that ripe time of life I am a schoolgirl—
a complete schoolgirl, and, on the whole very
happy in that capacity[.] It felt very strange at
first to submit to authority instead of exercising
it—to obey orders instead of giving them—but I
like that state of things—I returned to it with the
same avidity that a cow that has long been kept
on dry hay, returns to fresh grass—*
—Charlotte Brontë
to Ellen Nussey, May 1842

The journey abroad had begun. After an eleven hour
train ride to London, the group settled in for three days at the
Chapter Coffee House, not far from Saint Paul's Cathedral. On
Saturday, February 12, the rough ferry crossing to the European continent took fourteen hours. Charlotte became ill, but
Emily stayed on deck with waves crashing on the ship's side
and mist and spray in her face. A few days later, they were on
a stagecoach to Brussels. The next morning, Charlotte and

53

Emily, with their father, presented themselves at the Pensionnat Heger in the ancient quarter of the city.

They met the proprietors, Madame Zoë Heger, a small, pregnant, thirty-eight-year-old woman with auburn hair and a serene manner. Her husband, Monsieur Constantin Heger, a teacher at a boys' school—the Athenée Royale—next door, also gave literature lessons at his wife's school. Mme. Heger was efficient and capable. Her husband was intellectual and intense. He was five years younger than she and only seven years older than Charlotte.

The Reverend Brontë stayed in Brussels for one week, then set off for home. Charlotte and Emily settled into their studies with almost ninety other students. Soon the Hegers recognized their exceptional abilities, and Charlotte took special note of M. Heger. Charlotte wrote Ellen of her early impression of him:

> He is professor of rhetoric, a man of power as to mind, but very choleric and irritable as to temperament; a little black ugly being, with a face that varies in expression. Sometimes he borrows the lineaments of an insane tom-cat, sometimes those of a delirious hyena.

Little by little though, Charlotte began to admire, then to idolize Constantin Heger. Her studies with him were her first contact with honest and intelligent support for her writing. He helped her fine tune her work and urged her to strive toward a more elegant shape to it, commenting: "You must sacrifice, *without pity,* everything that does not contribute to clarity, verisimilitude and effect. Look with great suspicion on everything which sets off the main thought, so that the impression you give is highly coloured, graphic. . . . "

Emily, however, protested his method of teaching

In 1847 Zoë and Constantine Heger and their children sat for this portrait.

French, which required them to write essays in French in the styles of various French authors. M. Heger, years later, spoke of Emily to Mrs. Gaskell (Charlotte's biographer). He rated her genius as "something even higher" than Charlotte's. The force of this gift, he felt, was impaired by her "stubborn tenacity of will."

> She should have been a man—a great navigator. Her powerful reason would have deduced new spheres of discovery from the knowledge of the old; and her strong, imperious will would never have been daunted by opposition or difficulty; never have given way but with life.

Meanwhile, in March of 1842, Branwell had been dismissed from his railway position at Luddenden Foot. An audit revealed a deficit of eleven pounds. Though Branwell wasn't accused of stealing, he was deemed negligent in his duties. In fact, his journal reveals he spent much of his time writing and drawing and indulged in what he later referred to as "groveling carelessness."

Back at the parsonage, Branwell became friends with William Weightman, the curate. Several of Branwell's poems were published in various papers, including the *Bradford Herald.*

Then a blow struck. William Weightman, twenty-eight, died of cholera. The young curate who had brought so much joy and life to the parsonage was suddenly gone. Branwell and his father were both distraught, and the sisters also were deeply saddened at this unexpected passing of someone who had brought them so much happiness.

Then, to add even more sorrow to their lives, Aunt Branwell became seriously ill. Charlotte and Emily were summoned home from Brussels, but as they prepared to leave, a second telegram, black-bordered, arrived, telling of their aunt's death. The Hegers acknowledged that the Brontë girls needed to return home, but M. Heger expressed in a letter for their father his desire they would return:

> You will undoubtedly learn with pleasure that your children have made extra-ordinary progress in all the branches of learning, and that this progress is entirely due to their love of work and their perseverance. With pupils like this we had very little to do; their progress is more your work than ours.

He went on to suggest that one or both of the Brontës should return to Brussels to teach in the school.

When Charlotte and Emily arrived at the parsonage on November 8, 1842, they found that Branwell had been with both William Weightman and his aunt at the end. To ease his pain and despair, Branwell was increasing his dependence on alcohol—and on laudanum, a drug containing opium that was commonly prescribed at that time. He seemed to feel the brush of death's wings himself and was immersed in gloom.

It was decided that Emily would stay home and take over the role of housekeeper, a role she enjoyed. Tabby, who had left the parsonage in 1839 because of a lame leg, was summoned back to offer what help she could around the house. Charlotte would return to Brussels. Anne, who had come home briefly after her aunt's death, had already returned to Thorp Green. Anne also had obtained a position for Branwell there as a tutor to the Robinsons' eleven-year-old son, Edmund, to begin after the holidays.

Branwell brought new life to the family at Thorp Green with the engaging and bright side of his nature as he and Anne accompanied the Robinsons on holiday to the seaside resort of Scarborough. But, still mourning the deaths of two close to him, he may have been particularly vulnerable and open to sympathy. Perhaps it was here that Branwell was first drawn to Lydia Robinson, the mother of his charge.

Charlotte made the long journey back to Brussels alone on January 27, 1843. She was well received by the Hegers. As a teacher now—Mademoiselle Charlotte—she was even offered the use of their sitting room.

She taught English to the Belgian girls and to M. Heger and his brother-in-law, while she continued to learn French from M. Heger. He sometimes left gift books and notes in her desk—and the smell of smoke from his cigar remained to remind her of him.

Though Charlotte dared not admit it to herself, part of the reason she had wanted to return was to be near M. Heger. His intensity and intelligence had cast a spell on her. He had the ability to wither a pupil with a movement of his lip or exalt her with a flicker of his eyelid. And this was the man who encouraged Charlotte to write, urged her to perfect her gift. She now called him the black swan. Later a friend of the Hegers would write, "He made much of her, and drew her out & petted her, & won her love."

Charlotte gradually moved from feelings of respect for him to an unhealthy dependence on his approval. It was not long before Mme. Heger noticed and stopped contact between Charlotte and her husband. This left Charlotte feeling isolated and alone. She wrote:

> I am convinced she does not like me—why, I can't tell, nor do I think she herself has any definite reason for the aversion. . . . M. Heger is wondrously influenced by Madame . . . I fancy he has taken to considering me as a person to be let alone . . . I get on from day to day in a Robinson Crusoe-like condition—very lonely.

Charlotte plunged into a state of melancholy. She began to take long exhausting walks. During the summer vacation, she was left alone at the school for five weeks while students were away and the Hegers took their own vacation. She wandered into a Catholic cathedral and, despite her strong Protestant upbringing, confessed to a Catholic priest. "I felt as if I did not care what I did, provided it was not absolutely wrong, and that it served to vary my life and yield a moment's interest."

At home Emily was responsible for everything going smoothly at the parsonage. She was in charge of the kitchen and did all the heavy work, which Tabby was now too old to handle. She wrote poems again at the dining room table, read to her father, and played the piano for him. Mr. Brontë taught his unconventional daughter how to shoot and still insisted on discharging his own pistol each morning.

Finally, by December 1843, news that her father's eyesight was failing added to Charlotte's homesickness and isolation in Brussels and caused her to return to Haworth. In the end, her stay in Brussels had brought Charlotte great pain. She wrote Ellen on January 23, 1844:

> I think, however long I live, I shall not forget what the parting with M. Heger cost me—it grieved me so much to grieve him who had been so true and kind and disinterested a friend—

No matter how difficult it was, Charlotte's stay in Brussels enriched her life. Her disappointment in love, though painful, deepened her spirit. The visits to galleries, museums,

Ellen Nussey was Charlotte's good friend and faithful correspondent.

and the theater broadened her culturally. This time abroad helped her grow emotionally, intellectually, and artistically.

At home she found that though her father's eyesight continued to worsen, Branwell and Anne were both doing well at Thorp Green, and Emily was absorbed in her poems. She, herself, felt only a lack of energy.

By July 1844, Charlotte and Emily had worked out more details of the school they planned—The Misses Brontë's Establishment for the Board and Education of a Limited Number of Young Ladies/The Parsonage, Haworth. Charlotte would teach and Emily would attend to the housework. They could take five or six girls.

Charlotte wrote to friends and sent circulars to tell them of the plans, hoping this would bring students. But no students resulted, and there was great disappointment. Some families had felt the parsonage too remote, others felt the climate too damp. Charlotte wrote to her friend:

> Depend upon it Ellen, if you were to persuade a mamma to bring her child to Haworth—the aspect of the place would frighten her and she would probably take the dear thing back with her instanter[.] We are all glad that we have made the attempt and we are not cast down because it has not succeeded.

Charlotte could not forget her attachment to Constantin Heger. She had written him six long letters in French in the spring. One letter read, "You once showed me a little interest when I was your pupil in Brussels—and I cling on to preserving that little interest—I cling on to it as I cling to life." He replied with brief notes asking her please to write him only twice a year. She wrote, "Farewell my dear master—may God protect you with special care & crown you with peculiar blessings." His answer was silence.

In May 1845, Mr. Brontë acquired a new curate, a twenty-six-year-old Irishman, Arthur Bell Nicholls. Like the Reverend Brontë, Arthur came from an Irish farming family and was well educated. Charlotte and Emily were glad their father would have this help, but they showed little interest in Nicholls, the latest of several dull, uninteresting curates—always with the exception of William Weightman.

In June Anne came home from Thorp Green and announced she would not be returning. Anne wrote of her leaving in her diary of July 31, 1845: "During my stay I have had some very unpleasant and undreamt of experience of human nature." It is believed this related to Branwell, for when he came home, also in July of that year, he said he had been dismissed from the Robinsons.

Had Branwell had a love affair with Lydia Robinson? No one knows for sure what transpired—another mystery about Branwell—though evidence points in that direction. Gossip in Haworth was that the Robinsons' gardener had discovered Branwell and Mrs. Robinson together in a boathouse.

Not long after Branwell had arrived at Thorp Green in May 1843, he had written a friend:

> I curl my hair & scent my handkerchief like a Squire—I am the favourite of all the household—my master is generous—but my mistress is DAMNABLY TOO FOND OF ME. She is a pretty woman, about 37, with darkish skin & bright glancing eyes.

He asked his friend's advice on whether or not he should go on to "extremities," implying more intimacy with her. In October 1845, Branwell wrote another friend: "During nearly three years I had daily troubled pleasure soon chastised by fear in the society of one whom I must, till death call my wife." Anne, who obviously knew the reason for the dismissal, did not reveal it,

The Black Bull still serves food and drink in the town of Haworth,
just as in Branwell's day.

though it seemed clear her embarrassment or distress
regarding the situation was the reason she had left.

Whatever the truth, Branwell, back at Haworth and
deeply saddened, brooded and went still more heavily into
drink and laudanum. From time to time, he sent his friends
drawings decorated with gravestones and images of himself
being hanged. He spent many nights at the Black Bull and
days in bed. His father was stern with him, and even Emily
grew unsympathetic. Charlotte felt rage that he had turned
their home into a sort of hell.

Branwell's breakdown was the end of any more plans for
the Misses Brontë's Establishment. Charlotte even wrote
Ellen that she could not invite her to visit because of
Branwell's behavior. "I wish I could say one word to you in his
favour—but I cannot—therefore I will hold my tongue."

Branwell tried to rally his spirits to write, and during this time he developed the idea for a novel. His story of Maria Thurston, a neglected wife who yearns for love, seemed influenced by Mrs. Robinson. Perhaps this act of creativity gave Branwell some comfort as his life seemed to be falling apart.

The period, as full of turmoil as it was, brought all four Brontës home for the first time in years. It was the beginning of the sisters' years of literary fame.

*An artist imagined Charlotte, Anne, and Emily as they gathered
around the table to work on their poetry and to write their novels.*

EIGHT

"Never Was Better Stuff Penned"

They stirred my heart like the sound of a trumpet . . . I know no woman that ever lived ever wrote such poetry before. Condensed energy, clearness, finish—strange, strong pathos are their characteristics.

—Charlotte Brontë
to William Smith Williams,
September 1848

One day in October 1845, Charlotte was straightening things in the parlor when she discovered, near Emily's rosewood lap desk, two dark crimson, leather-bound manuscript books containing her sister's poems. Charlotte later wrote:

[S]omething more than surprise seized me,—a deep conviction that these were not common effusions, not at all like the poetry women generally write. I thought them condensed and terse, vigorous and genuine. To my ear, they had also a peculiar music—wild, melancholy and elevating.

As she looked over the poems, full of excitement, she scribbled beneath one, "Never was better stuff penned."

Immediately Charlotte thought to publish a volume of Emily's, Anne's, and her own poetry, to embark on careers as poets and pursue their destinies as writers.

But when Charlotte told Emily about her discovery and her ideas, Emily felt her privacy had been invaded. Charlotte later wrote, "It took hours to reconcile her to the discovery I had made, and days to persuade her that such poems merited publication."

Finally Emily agreed, and once Charlotte's plan was known, Anne brought out some of her own poems, too. Though Branwell was as prolific as his sisters and already had been published, he was not included. Presumably this was because of his mental state. Then, too, Branwell was very talkative. He would never have been able to keep their project a secret.

A new ritual began at the parsonage. After evening prayers, once their father wound the clock and went to bed and Branwell went out to his usual pubs, Emily, Charlotte, and Anne sat together at the dining table, reading aloud and discussing metaphor and meter. During the day, they continued to attend to the household duties of sewing, sweeping, ironing, and baking.

At last the book was ready: twenty-one poems each by Anne and Emily and nineteen by Charlotte. The three decided to disguise their gender. It was especially important to Emily and Anne to protect their privacy. Charlotte did not want to be considered a "silly lady scribbler," easily dismissed by the press of the day. She recalled Robert Southey's words: "Literature cannot be the business of a woman's life."

So they veiled their female identities under the names Currer (Charlotte), Ellis (Emily), and Acton (Anne) Bell.

Their surname was taken from Arthur Bell Nicholls, their father's latest curate.

Charlotte wrote to a number of publishers, who failed to respond. Then, one day, she sent a query to the firm of Aylott and Jones, booksellers and stationers, who published religious poetry and theological works. The firm agreed to publish the poems at the authors' expense, a fairly common practice in the nineteenth century. The sisters used part of a small inheritance from Aunt Branwell for costs.

Soon after, with the poems on the brink of publication, the sisters embarked on a new project. They each began a novel. Charlotte wrote to their publisher in April 1846 to inform them that they were now preparing three separate works of fiction but were not willing to pay for the publication of their books, as they had with the poems. The publisher declined publication.

All three worked on their novels as Charlotte looked for appropriate and willing publishers. Charlotte was writing *The Professor,* which reflected her stay in Brussels and her attraction to M. Heger. Emily was writing *Wuthering Heights,* a tale of the transcendent love of Catherine and Heathcliff, which included some characters from Gondal. *Agnes Grey,* by Anne, tells a realistic story of the life of a governess. It contains a character named Edward Weston, much like William Weightman, who marries Agnes and saves her from a governess's life. *Agnes Grey* and *The Professor* were probably examples of wish fulfillment. But not *Wuthering Heights.* The death-defying love of Catherine and Heathcliff was like a torrent of nature.

The sisters worked on their writing each night by the glow of the firelight. And separately Branwell too was working on a novel, which he decided to call "And the Weary Are

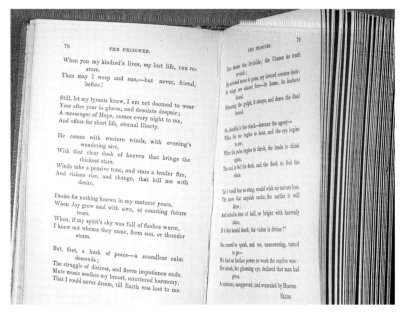

The first edition of Poems *by Charlotte, Emily, and Anne is opened to Emily's poem "The Prisoner."*

at Rest." It doesn't appear that Branwell and his sisters were aware of each other's endeavors.

In May 1846, copies of the slim green volume of *Poems* arrived at the parsonage. Charlotte made sure review copies were sent to a long list of magazines. Yet even then, the sisters did not share their cautious excitement with their brother or father. It remained their secret and their hope.

Later that month, the household was again upset when news came that Edmund Robinson, Branwell's former employer, had died. At first Branwell was jubilant, thinking this would lead him back to Lydia Robinson. As he prepared for a journey to Thorp Green to see Mrs. Robinson, he received a message that someone from Thorp Green wanted to see him at the Black Bull. He dressed hurriedly and walked quickly over to the pub, filled with joy. Sure enough, when he walked in, there was the Robinsons' coachman.

The coachman simply motioned for Branwell to follow him into a back room where they could be private. After a while the coachman left, and the barmaid continued clearing the bar and serving guests. She later described hearing a strange voice about an hour later "like the bleating of a calf." She rushed to the door of the room and found Branwell on the floor having a seizure.

The coachman had not brought Branwell the good news he hoped for. Instead he told him that Mr. Robinson had made a codicil (a later addition) to his will saying that his wife would be cut off from her inheritance and would have to give up her children if she ever saw Branwell again.

The truth is that Mr. Robinson's will did not even mention Branwell. Mrs. Robinson's purpose in sending that message for Branwell appears to have been to keep him from any rash acts, such as his plan to go to Thorp Green.

Amidst the gloom, and after two months with no reviews, suddenly two favorable reviews of *Poems* came out. One said, "[T]his small book of 170 pages only has come like a ray of sunshine, gladdening the eye with present glory and the heart with bright hours in store." But the reality was that only two copies of their book sold. Charlotte later wrote, "The mere effort to succeed has given a wonderful zest to existence, it must be pursued." In July of 1846, Charlotte started sending the three novels to London publishers.

Arthur Nicholls, who had been at the parsonage now for two years, was to be ordained. His ordination caused no ripples of interest in Charlotte or her sisters. Even so, there was talk in the parish that Charlotte and Mr. Nicholls might marry. Charlotte wrote to her friend Ellen:

> I scarcely need say that never was rumour more unfounded. . . . A cold far-away sort of civility are the only terms on which I have ever been with Mr. Nicholls—I could by no means think of mentioning such a rumour to him even as a joke—it would make me the laughing-stock of himself and his fellow curates for half a year to come—They regard me as an old maid, and I regard them, one and all, as highly uninteresting, narrow and unattractive specimens of the "coarser sex."

Charlotte had already turned down two marriage proposals. Now her energy and direction were focused on her writing and in helping her sisters become published.

The Reverend Brontë's eyesight continued to fail and he could no longer write nor read. He was able to continue to deliver sermons, however, after being led to the pulpit. In August Charlotte and Emily went to the city of Manchester, west of Haworth, to find a surgeon. Three weeks later, Charlotte returned with her sixty-nine-year-old father for his surgery. She stayed in the room, at his request, while the operation to remove his cataracts was performed without anesthesia, a grim ordeal for father and daughter.

Charlotte's heart was full of concern. She was worried about her father's sight and about Emily and Anne's ability to deal with Branwell. Even so, she started writing *Jane Eyre* the day after the surgery. The theme of a courageous and romantic governess telling her story directly to the reader had been growing in her mind. Now that she had solitude and quiet, she took out her pencil and wrote in little square paper books, held close to her eyes because of her shortsightedness, and let her imagination unfold.

She wrote at an exhilarating pace, even with pain from a toothache. At the same time, she nursed her father for the five weeks he had to remain in quiet seclusion in Manchester.

When the Reverend Brontë and Charlotte returned to the parsonage, his sight was restored and she was well into her novel. Many of Charlotte's personal experiences became part of the story. M. Heger was transported from Brussels to the halls and manor houses of her friends in the character of Rochester, the dark hero of the book. Cowan Bridge became Lowood, where Jane Eyre went to school. Her portrait of Bertha, Rochester's mad wife, had touches of Branwell's own madness. It also may have been drawn from a tale of a mad-woman locked in an attic that Charlotte heard while working as a governess or from a local story of an insane wife who lived on the edge of Haworth. Charlotte had come across the family name "Eyre" while traveling with Ellen, and the fif-teenth-century Eyre home may have been a model for Thorn-field Hall, Rochester's home.

Charlotte read the opening chapters to Emily and to Anne, who protested that Jane was not beautiful, and so not interesting. But petite Charlotte said she had created a hero-ine who was as small and plain as she was, and yet as inter-esting as her sisters' heroines. In truth, Anne had also created a plain heroine in *Agnes Grey.*

Not long after Charlotte and her father's return, chaos broke loose in the parsonage. One day the Reverend Brontë went out for a walk, and while he was gone, Anne discovered Branwell unconscious in his bed with the bed curtains on fire. He had apparently been drinking and knocked over his candle. Anne pulled on Branwell's arms, but she couldn't move him. Then Emily rushed in, dragged her brother into the corner of the room, pulled down the blazing bedding, and ran for a pail of water.

When their father returned to the house, he decided

Branwell must again sleep with him so that he could be watched over. Charlotte included a scene of Jane rescuing Rochester from a burning bed in *Jane Eyre.*

Perhaps Emily, to some extent, also wove Branwell into her own novel. The love of Catherine and Heathcliff may have been a reflection of Branwell's obsessive love for Lydia Robinson, and Hindley, Catherine's drunken brother, may also have been inspired by Branwell.

By the spring of 1847, Branwell was spending his time weaving unsteadily between the Black Bull and the druggist, buying alcohol and opium. No one knew how he was able to pay for it, but village gossip speculated that he received money regularly from Mrs. Robinson, perhaps to keep him at a distance and quiet.

Charlotte continued to work on *Jane Eyre,* interspersing her writing with domestic duties. She was full of energy and vitality during this time, even though there was still no publisher for *Wuthering Heights, Agnes Grey* and *The Professor.* The novels had been sent out over and over. Each time Charlotte merely marked off the name of the previous publisher on the wrapping paper and penned in the next.

The following month, a small firm, T. C. Newby, offered to publish *Wuthering Heights* and *Agnes Grey* but not *The Professor.* Newby would require that Emily and Anne pay fifty pounds toward production costs. Rather than risk never seeing their books in print, Emily and Anne agreed, again using money inherited from Aunt Branwell.

Charlotte continued to seek a publisher for her own book, next deciding to send it to an obscure London firm, Smith, Elder and Company. William Smith Williams, the firm's reader, declined the book but spoke encouragingly of Charlotte's writing—its "great literary power"—and asked to see her future works. Charlotte wrote back:

> I have a second narrative in 3 vols. now in progress
> and nearly completed to which I have endeavoured to
> impart a more vivid interest than belongs to the
> Professor; in about a month I hope to finish it—so that
> if a publisher were found for 'the Professor', the sec-
> ond narrative might follow as soon as was deemed
> advisable.... Will you be kind enough to favour me
> with your judgment on this plan.

Smith, Elder was unconvinced and declined Charlotte's

The first page of Charlotte's manuscript for Jane Eyre, *with her
pseudonym, Currer Bell, crossed out*

offer. Even so, less than three weeks later, in August 1847, Charlotte sent her recently completed *Jane Eyre* to them. The result was that Mr. Williams read it, then took it to George Smith, the publisher, who couldn't put it down. He canceled a horse ride with a friend and had lunch and dinner alone the day the manuscript was given to him. Later he recalled, "The next day we wrote to Currer Bell accepting the book for publication."

To Charlotte's great joy, six weeks later, on October 19, 1847, *Jane Eyre* was published without any expense on her

Jane meets Mr. Rochester in an illustration for Jane Eyre.

part. In her new book, Charlotte wrote from the female point of view, and though her earlier book *The Professor,* written from a male viewpoint, was somewhat autobiographical, *Jane Eyre* was even more a reflection of her life.

Jane Eyre received praise and excellent reviews. It was a sensation. One reviewer wrote:

> We wept over Jane Eyre. This, indeed, is a book after our own heart; and, if its merits have not forced it into notice by the time this paper comes before our readers, let us, in all earnestness, bid them lose not a day in sending for it. The writer is evidently a woman, and, unless we are deceived, new in the world of literature. But, man or woman, young or old, be that as it may, no such book has gladdened our eyes for a long while.

Jane Eyre enjoyed an almost immediate success in a way that few novels up to that time had. Sales soared. When William Makepeace Thackeray, Charlotte's favorite writer and the author of *Vanity Fair,* was sent a review copy, he wrote enthusiastically:

> I wish you had not sent me Jane Eyre. It interested me so much that I have lost (or won if you like) a whole day in reading it at the busiest period with the printers I know wailing for copy. . . . I don't know why I tell you this but that I have been exceedingly moved and pleased by Jane Eyre. It is a woman's writing, but whose? Give my respects and thanks to the author, whose novel is the first English one (and the French are only romances now) that I've been able to read for many a day.

The Reverend Brontë knew of *Jane Eyre* only after Charlotte took it, along with some of the favorable reviews, to his study one evening, and presented him with a copy. She recorded the scene.

> "Papa, I've been writing a book." "Have you, my dear?"
> and he went on reading. "But, Papa, I want you to look
> at it." "I can't be troubled to read ms." "But it is
> printed." "I hope you have not been involving yourself
> in any such silly expense." "I think I shall gain money
> by it. May I read you some reviews?"

Charlotte read him the reviews, then left him with a copy
of the book. Mr. Brontë invited his daughters to tea later that
day, and toward the end announced that Charlotte had written a book, "and I think it is a better one than I expected."

After this restrained response, the sisters didn't dare tell
him about the other books, published two months later, that
did not have such favorable reviews, for fear of how he might
react. In a way, they behaved in the same secretive way they
had as children when they wrote their tiny books in infinites-
imal print so that adults couldn't decipher their stories.

Thomas Newby hurriedly put *Wuthering Heights* and
Agnes Grey into print. He noted that there must be some link
between the now-famous Currer Bell and the Ellis Bell and
Acton Bell who had sent him their work.

The year 1848 brought recognition to all three Brontë sisters, though not all the notice was positive. Along with the
praise for *Jane Eyre*, there were other critics who were
shocked at the protagonist's unconventional attitudes, and
once Jane was referred to as a "brazen Miss."

There was much speculation about the mysterious Bells.
Some readers and critics thought all the books were written
by one person. *Agnes Grey* was the most likely to be ignored,
but even it received mild commendation by a few reviewers.

Wuthering Heights, on the other hand, received hostile
reviews. One critic declared:

A home on the moors, like this one, was the setting for Wuthering Heights.

> This is a strange book. It is not without evidences of considerable power; but, as a whole, it is wild, confused, disjointed, improbable; and the people who make up the drama, which is tragic enough in its consequences, are savages ruder than those who lived before the days of Homer.

Emily put away in her lap desk the five longest and most ambivalent reviews. Her genius and the harsh and powerful grandeur of her novel were not understood in her time.

Branwell's shattered personality still dominated the household, and it was in spite of the chaos he created that the sisters' novels were born. His seizures continued and his health was suffering. Anne wrote: "Branwell . . . has led us a sad life with his absurd and often intolerable conduct — Papa is harassed day and night—we have little peace—he is always sick, has two or three times fallen down in fits—what will be the ultimate end God knows."

Scholars now believe that all three sisters worked on second novels. Anne was writing *The Tenant of Wildfell Hall*.

Charlotte considered reworking *The Professor* and soon began *Shirley*. Emily probably also began a novel, since lost. Both Charlotte and Anne started second books before publication of their first, so it would seem likely Emily did also.

A letter from the publisher, Newby, found in Emily's lap desk, hints at this:

> 15 Feb. 1848 —
> Dear Sir,
>
> I am much obliged by your kind note & shall have great pleasure in making arrangements for your next novel. I would not hurry its completion, for I think you are quite right not to let it go before the world until well satisfied with it, for much depends on your new work[. If] it be an improvement on your first you will have established yourself as a first rate novelist.

George Smith, of Smith, Elder and Company, was Charlotte's publisher and friend.

It has been speculated that Charlotte may have destroyed the half-finished book after Emily's death. Charlotte once wrote, "Whether it is right or advisable to create beings like Heathcliff, I do not know. . . . I scarcely think it is." Charlotte was always very protective of Emily and wouldn't have wanted more criticism heaped on her sister's memory.

As *Jane Eyre* moved into its third printing, Charlotte began her third novel, *Shirley,* set during the time of the Luddite Riots (1811–1812), which her father had often spoken of. These riots involved hand loom and mill workers who had lost jobs because of the industrialization of the textile factories and were opposed to modern technology. Yet the starving and desperate Luddites are not central to Charlotte's plot. Instead she focuses on what she called "the condition of women," loosely basing her main character on Emily. Of her heroine she wrote, "she does not know her dreams are rare—her feelings peculiar."

By this time, Anne had finished *The Tenant of Wildfell Hall.* It drew a revealing portrait of the alcoholism she had observed in her brother. In some ways *The Tenant of Wildfell Hall* might be considered a response to *Wuthering Heights* (even the initials of the dwellings are the same—WH). But Anne's disruptive, uncouth hero hasn't the romantic attraction of the dark and difficult Heathcliff. Anne's novel shows how alcoholism can affect the lives of those who have to live with it, even the lives of the gentry and aristocracy, whom she had observed while working for the Robinsons. *The Tenant of Wildfell Hall* was published in June 1848 by T. C. Newby.

At this time, T. C. Newby began suggesting that Anne's books and *Wuthering Heights* were all written by the author of *Jane Eyre,* Currer Bell. He wanted to capitalize on the great success of *Jane Eyre* and had, in fact, sold the first sheets of

Anne's book to an American publisher as the latest work by Currer Bell. Smith, Elder's American correspondent wrote indignantly to complain. This information was sent to the sisters with "alarm, suspicion, and wrath" by Smith, Elder, who asked that the matter be cleared up. It was this misrepresentation by Newby that moved the indignant Charlotte and Anne to take the train to London to settle the situation.

After two days of being entertained by the Smiths and by Mr. Williams, the tired sisters returned to Haworth, but not before meeting with Newby and convincing him to cease misinforming the public about their identities. They also arranged to have the book of poems transferred to Smith, Elder. They were exhausted but secure in the fact that their separate identities as authors were maintained.

The Tenant of Wildfell Hall was praised almost as much as *Jane Eyre,* though there still were critics who condemned it for its realistic portrayal of alcoholism. One newspaper, the *Rambler,* claimed that, though it contained what they termed "disgusting scenes," it still wasn't as bad as *Jane Eyre.* "So revolting are many of the scenes," announced another paper, "that the reviewer to whom we entrusted it returned it to us, saying it was unfit to be noticed."

Despite or possibly because of the reviews, *The Tenant of Wildfell Hall* sold well, and a second edition was in preparation before the end of July. Charlotte, Emily, and Anne, under their pseudonyms, were now known literary figures, but at home their lives remained the same. There was still cleaning, mending, and ironing. And still they had to cope with the drunken rages and stupors of Branwell. That year Charlotte wrote to her friend Ellen: "Branwell is the same in conduct as ever—his constitution seems much shattered—Papa—and sometimes all of us have sad nights with him—he sleeps most of the day, and consequently will lie awake at night—But has not every house its trial?" Branwell was now suffering from fainting spells and frequent bouts of influenza. No one realized these illnesses masked tuberculosis.

This plaster medallion of Branwell is by his friend Joseph Bentley Leyland.

NINE

"Gone Like Dreams"

A year ago—had a prophet warned me how I should stand in June 1849—how stripped and bereaved—had he foretold the autumn, the winter, the spring of sickness and suffering to be gone through—I should have thought—this can never be endured.

—Charlotte Brontë
to William Smith Williams, 13 June 1849

Branwell was still sleeping in his father's room at night. Yet, even with the Reverend Brontë's careful concern, on September 22, 1848, just as summer ended and the cold winds began, Branwell went down to the village. He was found later in the day halfway up the lane toward the parsonage, too exhausted to walk. He was helped home by a neighbor.

Branwell had seen various doctors and talked openly of death, but his state of drunkenness had gone on so long that this most recent incident wasn't seen as critical. Only two days later, after being in bed one day, Branwell, at age thirty-one, was dead. He was conscious until near the end and struggled only briefly. His family was stunned—no one had realized how ill he had become.

Branwell made this sketch of a skeleton coming for a dying man just a few months before his own death.

Charlotte, who had been cold to her brother for two years, was too stricken even to attend the funeral. She collapsed and was incapacitated for a week, while Anne and Emily took care of her. Witnessing her brother's death had shocked her deeply. Though she lately had had little sympathy for him, she and Branwell had once been extremely close, creating Glass Town and Angria, and producing the little books. They had shared their artwork, their writing, their imaginations, and their childhoods.

The Reverend Brontë was devastated and refused to be comforted. Branwell had been his pride, his hope. Yet his unrealistic estimates of Branwell's talents had made his son's failures all the more painful and humiliating.

Charlotte wrote to William Smith Williams on October 2, 1848: "I do not weep from a sense of bereavement, . . . but for the wreck of talent, the ruin of promise, the untimely dreary extinction of what might have been a burning and shining light." A few weeks later, on November 8, Lydia Robinson married the newly widowed Sir Edward Scott.

Emily, Branwell's closest ally at home, had attended her brother's service, and afterward she became ill with what seemed like a cold. By late October, she had pain in her chest, shortness of breath, and a hacking cough. She was thin and white, yet refused to discuss her illness or to see a doctor. She said she would have no "poisoning doctor" near her. Emily retired at ten each night and came downstairs at seven each morning, even on the day of her death—panting, coughing, and holding her side in pain.

Charlotte abandoned her work, her new novel, *Shirley,* and worried as she observed her sister's haggard face and terrible pride. During this time of anxiety about Emily's illness, the sisters' volume of poetry was republished by Smith, Elder—and was dismissed by the critics.

As Emily grew sicker and weaker, a doctor was sent for, but she refused to see him. By the end of November, she could barely attend to her duties and was even too weak to read, yet she still stubbornly refused to take to her bed.

On Tuesday, December 19, she rose and dressed herself. She combed her hair before the fire, and when the comb slipped from her hand onto the hearth, she was too weak to pick it up. The partially burned comb is on display today at the parsonage.

Emily tried to take up her sewing but couldn't. She could only whisper in gasps, and her breath rattled. By midday she said, "If you will send for a doctor, I will see him now." But though the doctor came, it was too late. Around two o'clock that same day, Emily too died of tuberculosis.

Three days later, Emily's thin body was buried in the

vault with her mother, sisters Elizabeth and Maria, and Branwell. Mr. Nicholls conducted the service.

Mr. Brontë, Anne, and Charlotte followed the coffin to the grave. Tabby, a longtime member of the household, was there too. They were joined by Keeper, Emily's fierce, faithful dog. He walked alongside the mourners and into the church and stayed quietly there all the time the burial service was being read. When they came home, he lay down at Emily's chamber door and howled pitifully for many days.

The Reverend Brontë said to Charlotte almost hourly, "Charlotte, you must bear up—I shall sink if you fail me." Charlotte did "bear up" and did her best to comfort her father and sister.

Charlotte wrote often to William Smith Williams, who had become a kind confidant:

> 20 December 1848
> . . . Tuesday night and morning saw the last hours, the last agonies, proudly endured till the end. Yesterday Emily Jane Brontë died in the arms of those who loved her. . . . The last three months—ever since my brother's Death seem to us like a long, terrible dream. We look for support to God—

But the pain of loss was not over for Charlotte or her father. It wasn't long before the symptoms seen in Emily also appeared in Anne, as she too complained of pains in her side and came down with another bout of influenza. On January 5, only a brief two weeks after Emily's death, a respected doctor from Leeds, sent for by the Reverend Brontë, examined Anne, and confirmed she too was infected with tuberculosis.

Charlotte turned to nursing her last sister. Unlike Emily, Anne agreed to the various unpleasant remedies of the day: castor oil and blisters (hot compresses intended to draw the disease to the surface) applied to her side.

But when the physician discovered both lungs were affected, he reported there was little hope, though Anne's decline was gentler and less rapid than Emily's. Night after night, her cough was heard throughout the house, and she grew pale and thin.

Though Anne appeared to be handling her fate patiently and bravely, her anguish comes through in this verse from a poem she wrote at the time:

> A dreadful darkness closes in
> On my bewildered mind
> O let me suffer & not sin
> Be tortured yet resigned

Anne, thinking of her happy times at Scarborough with the Robinson family, felt that going to the sea was the one measure that might save her. When spring weather came, Charlotte, with her friend Ellen's help, prepared to grant Anne's wishes and take her to Scarborough. They booked lodgings in No. 2, The Cliff, where she had previously stayed with the Robinsons. The Reverend Brontë, and the servants, Tabby and Martha Brown, gathered to say good-bye to Anne. And then Anne caressed Emily's dog, Keeper, and her own little spaniel, Flossy.

Because they wanted the trip to seem like a holiday, they rented a donkey cart the day after they arrived in Scarborough. Anne even took the reins of the carriage for a while as they drove on the sand. On Sunday, May 27, she wanted to go to church but was talked out of it. The night passed and in the morning Anne got herself ready for the day. Around eleven, she spoke of feeling a change. She believed she had not long to live.

A physician was sent for, and he told her that the angel of death was near. After he left, Anne still sat in the chair and clasped her hands and prayed to God for a blessing, first upon Charlotte, then upon Ellen. Seeing that her sister could hardly restrain her grief, she said, "Take courage Charlotte! Take courage!"

At about two o'clock on Monday, the 28th of May, Anne died calmly and gently, conscious to the end. All the grief Charlotte had held inside for so many months overwhelmed her now, and it was not until the next day that she could recover some sense of calm. She wrote her father telling him of his youngest child's death and that she had decided to bury Anne at Scarborough, the place she had loved so much. Charlotte suggested he not come, to spare him the ordeal of seeing his fifth child buried.

The funeral was attended only by Charlotte, Ellen, and by Miss Wooler, the headmistress of Roe Head School, who lived

Anne Brontë's grave in Scarborough, the seaside town she loved

in the town. When she heard of the death, she came to give support to Charlotte, her former student and employee. The Reverend Brontë—alone in his study at Haworth—prayed for his daughter's soul while her body was put to rest seventy miles away.

Charlotte stayed in the area until the end of June, though she and Ellen moved ten miles down the coast to the less fashionable area of Filey. The gaiety of Scarborough was too painful to bear. In Filey Charlotte gazed out at the wild rocky coast and the solitary sands and looked for peace, "for life seems bitter, brief—blank," she wrote to William Smith Williams.

When Charlotte arrived home, all was clean and bright. Her father and the servants received her with great affection. But as she wrote to Mr. Williams:

> It is over. Branwell—Emily—Anne are gone like dreams—gone as Maria and Elizabeth went 20 years ago. One by one I have watched them fall asleep on my arm—and closed their glazed eyes—I have seen them buried one by one—and—thus far—God has upheld me. [F]rom my heart I thank Him.

Charlotte sat in the lonely parsonage aware of the ticking of the clock, remembering her siblings—the sharing of stories, the daily tasks, the walks on the moors. It was then she began to realize the importance of her work: "The fact is, my work is my best companion—hereafter I look for no great earthly comfort except what congenial occupation can give."

This crayon portrait of Charlotte by George Richmond was commissioned by George Smith.

TEN

Charlotte Alone

I am free to walk on the moors—but when I go out there alone—everything reminds me of the time when others were with me, and then the moors seem a wilderness, featureless, solitary, saddening. . . .

—Charlotte Brontë
to James Taylor, 22 May 1850

The years after Branwell's, Emily's, and Anne's deaths were Charlotte's years of celebrity, and yet they were years of loneliness and sorrow. That summer of 1849, after Anne's death, Charlotte, then thirty-three, passed many days alone in the dining room of the parsonage, where once she had talked, written, and spent the hours with her sisters.

Charlotte found the pain of bereavement almost unendurable, and so she did what she had always done in the past when faced with traumatic circumstances. She picked up her pen and refashioned reality. She turned to "making alive again," as they all had done since childhood.

91

Shirley, which had been set aside after Branwell's death and during Emily's and Anne's sicknesses and deaths, became her main interest and comfort. Besides being a tribute to Emily's memory—a portrayal of Emily as she might have been had she had health and prosperity—in *Shirley,* Charlotte created other characters, such as the three curates, based on people she knew, including Arthur Nicholls.

While Charlotte could now feel free to write under her true name—since her two very private sisters were gone—she chose to keep the protection of Currer Bell. She wrote to William Smith Williams that, in creating Currer Bell, she felt like "a wizard who had created a particularly powerful spirit."

When *Shirley* was finished at the end of August 1849, James Taylor, the manager at Smith, Elder offered to call at

An illustration of the main character from Charlotte Brontë's novel Shirley

Haworth on his way back from Scotland and take the manuscript to London. He arrived on September 8, and Charlotte took an immediate dislike to him. She wrote to Ellen, "He is not ugly—but very peculiar. . . . The lines in his face show an inflexibility and—I must add—a hardness of character which do not attract."

Shirley was published in October 1849 to mixed reviews, but it was a great popular success. By this time, most readers and critics knew Currer Bell was a woman. But despite its success, the reviews of Shirley were mostly disappointing to Charlotte. The review that appeared in the *Daily News* on October 31, 1849, especially bothered her.

> There are few things more forbidding than the commencement of a novel by the author of *Jane Eyre*. Like people who put dwarfs and monsters to keep their gates, or ugly dogs to deter idle folk from entering, so doth this writer manage to have an opening chapter or two of the most deterring kind. . . . The merit of the work lies in the variety, beauty, and truth of its female character.

Harriet Martineau and Mrs. Elizabeth Gaskell were two well-known authors of the day, and Charlotte sent a copy of Shirley to each of them. They did not know the identity of Currer Bell then, but both wrote admiring letters, which greatly pleased her. She replied to Elizabeth Gaskell on November 17, 1849: "Currer Bell <u>must</u> answer Mrs. Gaskell's letter—whether forbidden to do so or not—and She must acknowledge its kind, generous sympathy with all her heart."

William Makepeace Thackeray expressed a wish to meet the author of Shirley, so in November, Charlotte accepted an invitation from George Smith's mother to come to London—one of several trips she was to make in the next three years.

Of George Smith himself, Charlotte said, "He pleases me much; I like him better even as a son and brother than as a man of business."

At a dinner party at the Smiths', Charlotte met her hero Thackeray. And five days after meeting Thackeray, Charlotte also met Harriet Martineau, whose novel, *Deerbrook,* and essays on political economy she much admired.

At the parsonage, Mr. Brontë, who was proud of his daughter's achievements, revealed the true author of the books to Mr. Nicholls, his curate. Arthur read *Jane Eyre,* then was soon asking for *Shirley.*

The news spread throughout Haworth, and Charlotte could no longer walk invisible. The *Bradford Observer* stated,

The Brontës loved to wander these moors near Haworth.

"It is understood that the only daughter of the Rev P Brontë, incumbent of Haworth is the authoress of *Jane Eyre* and *Shirley*, two of the most popular novels of the day, which have appeared under the name of 'Currer Bell.'"

Soon Sir James Kay Shuttleworth, who made it his habit to know all important literary figures, invited Charlotte to spend a few days at his home. Charlotte found him overbearing, but she enjoyed the beauty of Gawthorpe Hall. When Mr. Brontë came down with a touch of bronchitis, however, Charlotte was glad to have an excuse to leave.

But back at home, she was ever aware of her deep losses. Even a walk on the moors brought sad thoughts.

> My sister Emily had a particular love for them, and there is not a knoll of heather, not a branch of fern, not a young bilberry leaf not a fluttering lark or linnet but reminds me of her. The distant prospects were Anne's delight, when I look round, she is in the blue tints, the pale mists, the waves and shadows of the horizon.

In June Charlotte visited London again, and during this visit she sat three times for a crayon portrait by the artist George Richmond—all arranged by George Smith, Charlotte's publisher. Charlotte burst into tears at the last sitting when the portrait was finished. She felt it looked like Anne. George Smith sent it to Mr. Brontë, and he hung it in the parsonage.

George Smith invited Charlotte to visit Edinburgh with him and his sister. Charlotte's friend Ellen was shocked, and George's mother disapproved—suspecting there was too much friendliness between the two, but Charlotte explained the relationship in a letter to Ellen:

> George and I understand each other very well—and respect each other very sincerely—we both know the wide breach time has made between us—we do not

George Richmond made this crayon portrait of Mrs. Elizabeth Gaskell, a writer who became Charlotte's friend and biographer.

embarrass each other, or very rarely—my six or eight years of seniority, to say nothing of lack of all pretense to beauty . . . are a perfect safeguard. . . .

But the difference in their ages and her lack of beauty did not keep them from enjoying each other's company. He referred often to her fine eyes and intelligence, and she was touched and flattered by his attention and charm.

Charlotte did travel to Scotland and spent two enjoyable days with George and his sister, Eliza Smith. But because of the disapproval of Ellen and George's mother, however, they did not go on beyond Edinburgh.

In August 1850, Charlotte again hesitantly accepted an invitation to visit the Kay Shuttleworths, this time at their home in Windermere, in the Lake District. Though she was reluctant to go, she longed to see the land of the Lake Poets. This visit was significant, for it was there she finally met the well-known author Mrs. Elizabeth Gaskell. Mrs. Gaskell was touched by Charlotte's loneliness, which she felt deeply when Charlotte told her what a companion the sky became to anyone living in solitude. Each went home with a pleasant feeling for the new acquaintance, and soon they were exchanging letters.

During this period, Smith, Elder decided to republish *Wuthering Heights* and *Agnes Grey,* which had been taken out of the hands of their original publisher. Charlotte was to prepare prefaces and biographical sketches of her sisters. She was happy to have Emily's and Anne's books under the umbrella of her own publisher.

As Charlotte looked again at *Wuthering Heights,* she was struck once more by its somber genius. She wrote, "It is rustic all through. It is moorish, and wild, and knotty as a root of heather."

She also edited both books severely in order to make them more acceptable to the public. She spoke of her sisters as naive artists who told the truth of the crudeness of the wild moors. "Neither Emily nor Anne was learned; they had no thought of filling their pitchers at the well-spring of other minds; they also wrote from the impulse of nature, the dictates of intuition, and from such stores of observation as their limited experience had enabled them to amass. . . . " Smith, Elder's editions of *Wuthering Heights* and *Agnes Grey* were published on December 10, 1850.

Charlotte made an attempt to brighten her surroundings by using some of the money she was earning from her writings to have the parsonage walls freshly painted. She even ordered curtains for the dining room, but then was not pleased with their bright crimson color. The emptiness couldn't be filled in spite of the trips and the attempt to redecorate. "There was a reaction that sunk me to the earth;" she wrote, "the deadly silence, solitude, desolation. . . . "

During that winter, Charlotte's life was complicated by James Taylor, the Smith, Elder manager, who had carried the manuscript of *Shirley* to London. He was to be sent to India, where he would head the Smith, Elder office. He asked permission to come to Haworth and then proposed to Charlotte and asked her to accompany him.

But something about him made her shrink. "Were I to marry him—my heart would bleed—in pain and humiliation—I could not—<u>could</u> not look up to him—No—if Mr. T be the only husband Fate offers to me—single I must always remain."

Charlotte knew her romantic heart could not be happy with him. After all, she had loved Constantin Heger, and now was fighting her feelings for George Smith.

During a visit to London in May 1851, George Smith took Charlotte to hear William Thackeray speak. She wrote her father:

> I have now heard one of Mr. Thackeray's lectures, and seen the Great Exhibition . . . the audience was composed of the very elite of London society—Duchesses were there by the score. . . . Amidst this Thackeray just got up and spoke with as much simplicity and ease as if he had been speaking to a few friends by his own fireside—The lecture was truly good.

George Smith later gave a different version of that evening. He and his mother had accompanied Charlotte to the lecture, and after it, Thackeray said out loud to his own mother, "Mother, you must allow me to introduce you to Jane Eyre."

> This was uttered in a loud voice, audible over half the room. Everybody near turned round and stared at the

> disconcerted little lady, who grew confused and angry
> when she realised that every eye was fixed upon
> her.... On the next afternoon Thackeray called. I
> arrived at home shortly afterwards, and when I
> entered the drawing-room found a scene in full
> progress. Only these two were in the room. Thackeray
> was standing on the hearthrug, looking anything but
> happy. Charlotte Bronte stood close to him, with head
> thrown back and face white with anger.... The spec-
> tacle of this little woman, hardly reaching to Thack-
> eray's elbow, but, somehow, looking stronger and
> fiercer than himself, and casting her incisive words at
> his head, resembled the dropping of shells into a
> fortress.

Once Charlotte was home, she was again beset with loneliness. She found it hard to begin another book, though
Smith, Elder waited and encouraged her. In December the
death of Keeper, Emily's dog, echoed the great losses of
Charlotte's siblings three years before.

Finally she took up her pen. Again she decided to base a
novel on her experience in Brussels. But unlike *The Professor,*
this book would benefit from the eight years that had passed.
And while *The Professor* was from the male point of view,
Villette would have as its center a young woman, Lucy Snowe.
Perhaps, with distance, Charlotte could take apart the pieces
of her time in Brussels—her attraction to Constantin Heger,
the object of her unrequited love, and her loneliness—and
fully develop these themes. So, in 1851, she began her fourth
and last complete novel, *Villette,* the story of a young teacher
in Brussels and the schoolmaster with whom she falls in love.

In early summer, her father suffered a slight stroke and
it was feared he would lose his sight again. Charlotte cared
for him, and soon the partial paralysis he suffered disap-
peared, though one of his eyes was inflamed for a month and

Lucy Snowe and Paul Emanuel, in an illustration from Villette

activated his fears of blindness. Once more Charlotte was trying to write a book while nursing her father.

She continued to work on *Villette,* however, and longed for someone to discuss it with. For the first time, Charlotte was writing a book without the exchange of ideas the Brontë siblings had always loved. In October she wrote George Smith:

> I can hardly tell you how much I hunger to have some opinion besides my own, and how I have sometimes desponded and almost despaired because there was no one to whom to read a line—or of whom to ask a counsel. "Jane Eyre" was not written under such circumstances, nor were two-thirds of "Shirley". I got so miserable about it, I could bear no allusion to the book . . . it is not finished yet, but now—I hope.

She sent the unfinished manuscript to George Smith, and within a week of reading it, he expressed his approval. He even recognized himself in the character of Dr. John Bretton. Charlotte was so pleased that some of her old gaiety returned. As to the fate of Dr. John, Charlotte wrote: "[H]e is far too youthful, handsome, bright spirited and sweet tempered; he is a 'curled-darling' of Nature and of Fortune . . . his wife must be young, rich and pretty; he must be made very happy indeed."

On November 10, 1852, Charlotte finished the third volume of *Villette.* She was thirty-six and facing life with no sisters, no brother, and without a mate.

Villette was published in January of 1853. It is the story of Lucy Snowe, a teacher who goes to Brussels, where many of her experiences were taken from Charlotte's memories of the Pensionnat Heger. While her feelings for M. Heger are part of the book in the character of Paul Emanuel, she also includes the portrait of George Smith as Doctor John.

Villette is a mature exploration of loneliness, depression, and suffering, with the insight into them Charlotte had gained over the years. And because her feelings for Constantin Heger are such an important part of the story, it has been called the longest love letter ever written.

Arthur Bell Nicholls, one of Patrick Brontë's curates at Haworth Church, was a devoted admirer of Charlotte for many years.

ELEVEN

Charlotte and Mr. Nicholls

*That he cared something for me—and wanted me
to care for him—I have long suspected—but I did
not know the degree or strength of his feelings.*
—Charlotte Brontë
to Ellen Nussey, 15 December 1852

Arthur Nicholls had been at the parsonage since 1846, the year of Branwell's dismissal by the Robinsons. He was around during the threat of Mr. Brontë's blindness and during Branwell's and Emily's deaths. Charlotte saw him everyday. She once described him to Ellen as good and mild—but she never seemed to have much interest in him. Yet all along he had been her silent and devoted admirer.

One Monday evening in December 1852, while Mr. Nicholls was at tea with Charlotte and the Reverend Brontë, Charlotte noticed he was constantly gazing at her with what she described as "strange, feverish restraint." After tea she went to the dining room and he followed her there. "Shaking from head to foot, looking deadly pale, speaking low, vehemently yet with difficulty—he made me for the first time feel what it costs a man to declare affection where he doubts response."

Charlotte was touched by his ardor and insecurity. She realized Mr. Nicholls was as capable of suffering and passion as she was. "I could only entreat him to leave me then and promise a reply on the morrow. I asked him if he had spoken to Papa. He said—he dared not—I think I half-led, half put him out of the room."

After he left, Charlotte went to her father to report on Arthur's visit. Mr. Brontë was immediately agitated and angered, horrified that his curate would dare ask for the hand of his daughter, his last remaining child. He persuaded Charlotte to give a firm refusal.

Was it that he feared losing his last child? Or did he feel his daughter deserved someone more distinguished? Was it because he was trying to forget his own humble Irish beginnings? Mr. Nicholls was, after all, an Irishman of hardworking ancestry. Or did he fear for Charlotte in childbirth?

From then on, Mr. Brontë referred to the proposal as "that obnoxious subject." He pitilessly attacked Mr. Nicholls, who took sanctuary in his room, pined, and refused meals, horrifying his landlady. The only creature to visit him daily was Anne's dog, Flossy.

With passions running oo high at home, Charlotte sought refuge in an invitation from Mrs. Smith, the publisher's mother, to visit London before the publication of *Villette*. She was beginning to sense, though, that Mrs. Smith's and George's kindnesses to her were for business rather than personal reasons.

Villette was published in January 1853 and received almost universal praise. Charlotte was a great success as an author. A review in the *Literary Gazette,* February 5, 1853, noted:

This book would have made her famous, had she not been so already. It retrieves all the ground she lost in *Shirley,* and it will engage a wider circle of admirers than *Jane Eyre,* for it has all the best qualities of that remarkable book.

But Harriet Martineau, whom Charlotte greatly admired and by whom she had felt appreciated, disliked the book and was offended by its emphasis on passion and love. She attacked the book first in a letter and then in the *Daily News.*

All the female characters, in all their thoughts and lives, are full of one thing, or are regarded by the reader in the light of that one thought—love ... —so incessant is the writer's tendency to describe the need of being loved, ...

This offended Charlotte so much she ended the friendship. She wrote Harriet, "I know what <u>love</u> is as I understand it; and if man or woman should be ashamed of feeling such love, then there is nothing right, noble, faithful, truthful, unselfish in this earth." The rift between the two literary women never healed.

Arthur was so hurt by the refusal of his offer of marriage and by Mr. Brontë's wrath that he resigned his curacy and offered himself as a missionary to the Australian colonies. Charlotte was in despair about Arthur.

He & Papa never speak. He seems to pass a desolate life.... He sits drearily in his rooms—If Mr Cartman or Mr Grant or any other clergyman calls to see and as they think to cheer him—he scarcely speaks—I find he tells them nothing—seeks no confidant ... I own I respect him for this.... We never meet nor speak—nor dare I look at him—silent pity is just all I can give him—

Charlotte again escaped the discomfort of the situation by going to visit her friend Mrs. Gaskell in April. She thoroughly enjoyed herself, and it cemented the friendship of the two authors. When Charlotte returned to Haworth, Mr. Nicholls only had a month left before his position there came to an end. On his last morning, as he was serving Communion, he reached Charlotte with the wafer. Then, according to Charlotte: "He struggled— faltered—then lost command over himself—stood before my eyes and in the sight of all the communicants white, shaking, voiceless—Papa was not there— Thank God!"

Later, after receiving an inscribed gold watch and a send-off by the parishioners, Mr. Nicholls called at the parsonage to say good-bye to the Reverend Brontë. As he left, Charlotte noticed he stood by the gate for a long time, and remembering his grief, she went out, trembling herself. "I found him leaning against the garden door . . . sobbing as women never sob. Of course I went straight to him. Very few words were interchanged—those few barely articulate: . . . Poor fellow!"

Not long after Arthur Nicholls left, Mrs. Gaskell came to visit. She was impressed with the tidiness and warmth of the parsonage in spite of the bleak surroundings. Mrs. Gaskell had a preconceived dislike for the Reverend Brontë, and she found these feelings were confirmed.

> He was very polite and agreeable to me; . . . but I was sadly afraid of him in my inmost soul; for I caught a glare of his stern eyes over his spectacles at Miss Brontë once or twice . . . and Miss Brontë never remembers her father dressing himself in the morning without putting a loaded pistol in his pocket, just as regularly as he puts on his watch.

According to Juliet Barker, former curator and librarian of the Brontë Parsonage Museum and biographer of the family, "It was unfortunate that Mrs. Gaskell met Patrick at the one time when he had exercised his parental authority and, as a result, his relationship with his daughter was at its lowest point ever." Barker states that Mrs. Gaskell drew broad conclusions and saw Patrick as a tyrant.

In December Charlotte learned of George Smith's engagement. Her curt note to him reveals the feeling of loss she must have experienced—since she had always enjoyed his company even though she always claimed nothing would come of it. Charlotte wrote her publisher and friend:

> My dear Sir
> In great happiness as in great grief—words of sympathy should be few. Accept my meed [an earned reward] of congratulation—and believe me
> Sincerely yours
> C. Brontë

After he left, Arthur began to write to Charlotte. He persevered even though six letters went unanswered. And then perhaps out of pity—after all Charlotte knew what it was to wait for letters—she was drawn into correspondence. She also began to value the steadfastness of his attachment to her and wanted to get to know him better. Charlotte finally confessed the correspondence to her father.

She insisted that the love of this good and ordinary man be given a chance. He was coming in January to the nearby village of Oxenhope and could take the footpath to Haworth. So the two had meetings to which her father reluctantly agreed. Charlotte wrote: "[A]ll I learnt inclined me to esteem, and if not love—at least affection."

Though Arthur Nicholls didn't fit Charlotte's ideal of a

romantic figure, she became convinced of his loyalty, devotion, and moral worth. He was connected to her past—and to her future. She could continue her commitment to her home and her father with him. Charlotte decided she could make him happy, and she said his love was too good to be thrown away by one as lonely as she was.

The Reverend Brontë at last gave his consent for the marriage. Arthur Nicholls wrote the Missionary Society a final letter, saying that he was giving up any plan to go abroad. Charlotte's letter to Ellen tells the tale:

> In fact, dear Ellen, I am engaged. Mr Nicholls in the course of a few months will return to the curacy of Haworth. I stipulated that I would not leave Papa—and to Papa himself I proposed a plan of residence. . . . What seemed at one time—impossible—is now arranged—and Papa begins really to take a pleasure in the prospect.

Charlotte and Arthur were officially engaged in April 1854, and preparations for the marriage were begun. Charlotte made purchases in Leeds for the wedding. She arranged for painting and wallpapering in the parsonage, and she had the little pantry behind the dining room converted into a study with green and white wallpaper and curtains for her new husband.

The day before the wedding, her friends Ellen Nussey and Miss Wooler arrived for the ceremony—and Charlotte arranged carefully for her father's comfort while she was away on the honeymoon. But on the night before the wedding, Mr. Brontë unexpectedly announced he could not give Charlotte away. He would not go to the church. Perhaps he could not face giving up his last child, but Charlotte believed his plea of poor health.

*Charlotte Brontë in 1854,
the year she was married*

It was her former teacher and employer, Margaret Wooler, who saved the day. She diplomatically agreed to step in and give Charlotte away. Ellen would be Charlotte's bridesmaid.

At 8 A.M. on June 29 in 1854, eighteen months after the trembling proposal, Charlotte and Arthur were wed in her father's church. Martha Brown, the housekeeper, raided village gardens to decorate the house with bouquets, and Ellen scattered flowers in the bride's honor at the wedding breakfast. After the ceremony and breakfast, Charlotte and Arthur started off for a six-week stay in Ireland, traveling from Dublin to Banagher to visit Arthur's family, the Bells, at their elegant family home, Cuba House.

Charlotte was impressed with her new Irish relatives, who were, she said later, "thoroughly educated gentlemen." Charlotte was also touched by the constant attention Arthur paid to her. She said that "kind and ceaseless protection" surrounded her and made traveling different than it had ever been for her before. Mr. Nicholls became "Arthur," then "my dear Arthur," and then "my dear boy." Charlotte wrote to Miss Wooler:

> My dear husband too appears in a new light here in his own country. More than once I have had deep pleasure in hearing his praises on all sides. Some of the old servants and followers of the family tell me I am a most fortunate person for that I have got one of the best gentlemen in the country.

When they returned to Haworth on August 1, they became immersed in busy daily parish life. Mr. Brontë was ill and Charlotte nursed him back to health. Arthur quietly took over many of the duties of the parish, and he insisted Charlotte share in everything he did. She wrote to Miss Wooler: "My own life is more occupied than it used to be: I have not so much time for thinking: I am obliged to be more practical, for my dear Arthur is a very practical as well as a very punctual methodical man. . . . "

Ellen began to resent Arthur, partly because of the intimacy she had lost with Charlotte—but mostly she could not forgive his interference in their correspondence. In an unguarded moment, Charlotte had written to her:

> Arthur has just been glancing over this note—He thinks I have written too freely. . . . I'm sure I don't think I have said anything rash—however, you must <u>burn</u> it when read. Arthur says such letters as mine never ought to be kept— they are dangerous as lucifer matches. . . . I can't help laughing—this seems to me so funny. . . . he is bending over the desk with his eyes full of concern.

Then Anne's little dog, Flossy, died almost three years to the day that Keeper, Emily's dog, had died. And Tabby, the faithful servant, became seriously ill. Yet even with these concerns and her new duties, Charlotte began a new novel, "Emma," about a plain heroine who poses as a woman of wealth. But Charlotte only wrote a few chapters over several months, and it was never finished.

On November 29, Charlotte was getting ready to write Ellen when Arthur, who loved fresh air and long walks, asked her to walk on the moors with him. It began to rain as they were returning home and they both arrived drenched.

That same night, Charlotte came down with a cold. Then she grew ill with nausea, faintness, and fever and had to be confined to her bed. In January she wrote to Ellen:

> My health has been really very good ever since my return from Ireland till—about 10 days ago, when the stomach seemed quite suddenly to lose its tone—indigestion and continual faint sickness have been my portion ever since. Don't conjecture—dear Nell—for it is too soon yet—though I certainly never before felt as I have done lately. But keep the matter wholly to yourself—for I can come to no decided opinion at present.

Her letter seems to suggest the classic symptoms of morning sickness. Charlotte Brontë was pregnant, but there was nothing normal about her intense illness. On February 17, Charlotte, still expecting to recover, wrote out her will, leaving everything to Arthur. She trusted him totally and knew he would care for her father. That very day, Tabby died at eighty-four years of age.

Soon Charlotte was vomiting heavily and the vomit was mixed with blood. By the second week in March, she was so weak she could not hold a pencil to write. She slipped into a delirium in which she constantly craved food and drink. Once she awakened and saw Arthur praying at her bedside. "'Oh,' she whispered forth, 'I am not going to die, am I? He will not separate us, we have been so happy.'"

On March 31, 1855, only nine months after their marriage, Arthur wrote to Ellen, "Our dear Charlotte is no more— She died last night of Exhaustion." The cause of death was listed as pthisis, indicating a progressive wasting disease, such as tuberculosis, but there is little doubt that Charlotte had died of *hyperemesis gravidarum,* excessive vomiting during pregnancy. Her unborn child died with her. She would have been thirty-nine in three weeks.

Ellen Nussey had hurried to the parsonage, but by the time she arrived, Charlotte was already gone. Martha, the housekeeper, brought Ellen a tray of evergreens to lay on the body. The memory of the flowers at the wedding breakfast almost prevented her from performing this loving duty.

On Wednesday, April 4, 1855, Charlotte's funeral was held. The church and churchyard were crowded with parish-

The village of Haworth, nestled in the moors, became famous as the home of the Brontë sisters.

ioners. The Brontë sisters, especially Charlotte, had made the little village of Haworth famous.

The minister who had performed Charlotte and Arthur's marriage nine months before performed the funeral service as well and committed Charlotte's body to the family vault. Ellen Nussey left an hour after the funeral. She recalled later, bitterly, that Arthur had on the day of her arrival said to her, "Any letters you may have of Charlotte's you will not shew to others & in course of time you will destroy them." Fortunately, Ellen did not obey Arthur's demand, for it is largely because of those letters that today we are able to piece together the story of this incredible family. Mr. Brontë wrote to Mrs. Gaskell April 5, 1855:

> I thank you for your kind sympathy—My daughter, is indeed, dead, and the solemn truth presses upon her worthy, and affectionate Husband and me, with great, and, it may be with unusual weight—But others, also, have, or shall have their own sorrows, and we feel our own the most—The marriage that took place, seem'd to hold forth, long, and bright prospects of happiness, but in the inscrutable providence of God, all our hopes have ended in disappointment, and our joy in mourning.

Epilogue

The myths and legends about Charlotte Brontë began as soon as she was buried.

She was called by Harriet Martineau in the *Daily News* a "frail little creature" and her father "too much absorbed in his studies to notice her occupations." Her home in the wild Yorkshire hills was viewed as "a place where newspapers were never seen."

She was also described as "morbidly sensitive," having the "patience of a hero, the conscientiousness of a saint." Her home was "a forlorn house" and a "living sepulchre." Her true intellectual, spirited—sometimes cynical—nature was buried beneath this melodramatic portrait of her life.

A very gossipy article appeared in *Sharpe's London Magazine,* again with a grim portrayal of her home and father. Ellen Nussy was especially angered by this one and brought it to the Reverend Brontë's attention in June 1855, suggesting a biography be written to tell the true story.

It was then that the Reverend Brontë contacted Mrs. Gaskell to ask her to write the story of his famous, much loved daughter. The irony is that the particular article that incensed Ellen had quoted extensively from Mrs. Gaskell's own letters after first meeting Charlotte in the Lake District in 1850. They were based on the gossip Lady Kay Shuttleworth had received from the only servant to be dismissed from the Brontë household.

Mrs. Gaskell began gathering material. Ellen gave her more than three hundred of the five hundred letters from Charlotte that she had saved. Mr. Nicholls turned over a dozen letters, mostly written to Emily and other family members. Miss Wooler, at first reluctant to give up her letters, finally agreed after a visit from Mrs. Gaskell. George Smith, too, reluctantly acquiesced after several letters and a visit. Evidently Mrs. Gaskell could be quite persuasive, for he even surrendered letters he had felt were too personal.

Ellen was especially eager to participate and not only made her letters available, but her opinions and prejudices as well. Mrs. Gaskell listened to her and accepted Ellen's versions of Charlotte's life, rather than interview Charlotte's father and husband again. Perhaps she wanted to spare them the pain, but by neglecting their observations and memories, she was less able to paint a balanced portrait of Charlotte.

Mrs. Gaskell even went to Brussels to interview the Hegers. Though Mme. Heger refused to see her, Constantin Heger met with her and gave her the essays written by both Charlotte and Emily, and he even carefully transcribed selected portions from Charlotte's letters to him. Mrs. Gaskell respected him and, as a result, tried to protect his, and Charlotte's, reputation by glossing over Charlotte's estrangement from Mme. Heger and the reasons for her departure.

Mrs. Gaskell went to the parsonage again, armed with the presence of Sir James Kay Shuttleworth. He used his powers of persuasion to obtain from the Reverend Brontë and Arthur the letters and manuscripts Mrs. Gaskell still needed for the book. They also took back with them another treasure, a container full of the little books written in childhood.

Mr. Brontë was unaware that as Mrs. Gaskell wrote the book of Charlotte's life, she included the cruel anecdotes about him that she heard from Ellen. In fact, he trusted her so much he did not ask to see the finished manuscript.

The Life of Charlotte Brontë was published by Smith, Elder and Company on March 25, 1857, in a two-volume set. It created a sensation not unlike the publication of *Jane Eyre*.

When Mr. Brontë read the book, he wrote a letter of praise to its publisher, George Smith. Only as an afterthought, he added, "There are a few trifling mistakes which, should it be deem'd necessary, may be corrected in the second edition."

Mr. Brontë later wrote Mrs. Gaskell, "I do not deny that I am somewhat excentric. Had I been numbered amongst the calm, sedate, *concentric* men of the world, I should not have been as I now am, and I should, in all probability never have had such children as mine have been."

The Professor was finally published posthumously in June 1857, but its acceptance was pale compared to *Jane Eyre, Wuthering Heights, The Tenant of Wildfell Hall,* and Mrs. Gaskell's *The Life of Charlotte Brontë.*

A fifty-page fragment of Charlotte's last, unfinished, novel, "Emma," was published by George Smith in *Cornhill,* a magazine he founded. It appeared in the March 1860 issue as "The Last Sketch,"—with an introduction by Thackeray.

On October 30, 1859, the Reverend Brontë preached his last sermon. He died on June 7, 1861. All the shops in Haworth closed on the day of his funeral, and hundreds of people came to pay their respects.

The connection with the Brontës at the parsonage was broken. Arthur was not asked to be the new minister. He was given this harsh news three months after Mr. Brontë's death and took it with his usual dignity and silence, though he had lost everything and had nowhere to go, except back home to Ireland.

He was, however, determined to preserve as many as possible of the Brontë belongings, so he took what he could, including manuscripts, letters, Emily's and Anne's diary papers, the rest of the tiny childhood books, some of

Charlotte's clothing, and the writing desks. Other items were sold at auction.

A month later, Arthur, accompanied by the housekeeper, Martha Brown, moved to Ireland to live with an aunt. He never again sought a clerical position but instead became a farmer. In 1864 he married Mary Bell, his cousin. They had no children, and his wife understood the devotion Arthur always felt for Charlotte.

Arthur died on December 2, 1906, at the age of eighty-eight and was buried in the churchyard at Banagher. His wife, short of money, sold the Brontë items at auction.

The Brontë Society was formed in 1893 in an effort to collect and preserve family belongings. In 1928 the Haworth parsonage was bought by a local businessman and presented to the Society. It was opened to the public as the Brontë Parsonage Museum.

Jane Eyre and *Wuthering Heights* continue to be two of the most widely read books in the English language, and the books by the Brontës have been published all over the world. Hundreds of plays and films have been written based on their lives and their novels. Each year one hundred thousand visitors stop at the parsonage in the Yorkshire village of Haworth to see firsthand the home of this family of geniuses who lived on the moors.

The four Brontë siblings made use of deep wells of imagination to embellish and enrich their simple and difficult lives and to create their novels and poetry. The freedom they found in the moors, along with the hard realities of their day-to-day existence, gives an energy to their works that keeps them very much alive.

Sources

p. 7   Charlotte Brontë to W. S.
       Williams, 29 August 1849.
       Quoted in Juliet Barker, *The
       Brontës: A Life in Letters*
       (Woodstock and New York:
       The Overlook Press, 1998),
       196.

p. 11 Charlotte Brontë to Mary
       Taylor, 4 September 1848.
       Quoted in Barker, 1998, 196.

p. 12 George Smith, *A Memoir with
       Some Pages of Autobiography,*
       1902. Quoted in Lyndall
       Gordon, *Charlotte Brontë: A
       Passionate Life* (New York and
       London: W. W. Norton and
       Co., 1994), 168.

p. 12 Charlotte Brontë to Mary
       Taylor, 4 September 1848.
       Quoted in Barker, 1998, 196.

p. 13 Ibid., 198.

p. 15 Cathal O'Byrne, *The Gaelic
       Source of the Brontë Genius.*
       (Folcroft, PA: Folcroft
       Library Editions, 1933,
       1969).

p. 17 Elizabeth Gaskell to
       Catherine Winkworth, 25
       August 1850. Quoted in
       Barker, 1998, 104.

p. 21 Branwell Brontë, *The Poems
       of Patrick Branwell Brontë.*
       Tom Winnifirth, ed. (Oxford:
       Blackwell, 1983), n.p.

p. 27 Christine Alexander. *The
       Early Writings of Charlotte
       Brontë* (New York:
       Prometheus Books, 1983), 31.

pp. 28–29 Charlotte Brontë, "The
       History of the Year," *MS Bon*
       80, 11 (1829): 4. Quoted in
       Juliet Barker. *The Brontës.*
       (London: Weldenfield and
       Nicolson, 1995), 154.

p. 33 "Charlotte Brontë," *MS Bon* 98, 8
       (1836): 1–2. Quoted in Barker
       1995, 254.

p. 34 Mary Taylor to Elizabeth Gaskell,
       18 January 1856. Ibid., 172.

p. 37 Charlotte Brontë, poem written
       19 December 1835. Quoted in
       Brian Wilks, *The Brontës* (New
       York: The Hamlyn Publishing
       Group, Ltd., 1976), 50.

p. 38 Charlotte Brontë, preface to *A
       Selection of Poems by Ellis Bell,* by
       Emily Brontë (Philadelphia: Lea
       and Blanchard, 1850). Quoted in
       Barker, 1995, 236.

p. 40 Robert Southey to Charlotte
       Brontë, March 1837. Quoted in
       Barker, 1998, 47–48.

p. 40 Charlotte Brontë to Robert
       Southey, 16 March 1837. Ibid.,
       48–49.

p. 43 Charlotte Brontë to Ellen Nussey,
       3 March 1841. Quoted in Barker,
       1995, 351.

p. 44 Charlotte Brontë to Ellen Nussey,
       12 March 1839. Ibid., 301.

p. 46 Charlotte Brontë to Emily Jane
       Brontë, 8 June 1839. Ibid.,
       310–311.

p. 46 Emily Jane Brontë. "Well, Some
       May Hate and Some May Scorn."
       14 November 1838. Ibid., 317.

p. 47 Charlotte Brontë to Ellen Nussey,
       4 August 1839. Barker, 1995, 314.

p. 48 Charlotte Brontë to Ellen Nussey,
       20 January 1842. Ibid., 366.

p. 50 Emily Jane Brontë, *The Complete
       Poems of Emily Jane Brontë*
       (London: Penguin Classics,
       1992), 30.

p. 51 Charlotte Brontë to Elizabeth
       Branwell, 29 September 1841.
       Quoted in Barker, 1995, 362.

p. 53 Charlotte Brontë to Ellen Nussey, May 1842. Quoted in Barker, 1998, 101.

p. 54 Charlotte Brontë to Ellen Nussey, May 1842. Quoted in Barker, 1995, 383.

p. 54 Constantin Heger, 30 April 1842. Ibid., 391.

p. 55 Constantin Heger to Mrs. Gaskell, 1856. Ibid., 392.

p. 56 Constantin Heger to Patrick Brontë, 5 November 1842. Ibid., 405.

p. 58 Mr. Westwood to unknown, 21 November 1869–21 February 1870. Ibid., 419.

p. 58 Charlotte Brontë to Emily Jane Brontë, 29 May 1843. Quoted in Barker, 1998, 115–116.

p. 58 Charlotte Brontë to Emily Jane Brontë, 2 September 1843. Quoted in Barker, 1995, 423.

p. 59 Charlotte Brontë to Ellen Nussey, 23 January 1844. Ibid., 427.

p. 60 Charlotte Brontë to Ellen Nussey 14 November 1844. Ibid., 123.

p. 60 Charlotte Brontë to Constantin Heger, 8 January 1845. Ibid., 444.

p. 60 Charlotte Brontë to Constantin Heger, 18 November 1845. Quoted in Gordon, 120.

p. 61 Anne Brontë, Diary Papers, 31 July 1845. Quoted in Barker, 1995, 455.

p. 61 Patrick Branwell Brontë to John Brown, May 1845. Ibid., 459.

p. 61 Patrick Branwell Brontë to Francis Grundy, October 1845. Quoted in Barker, 1998, 137.

p. 62 Charlotte Brontë to Ellen Nussey, 4 November 1845. Quoted in Barker, 1995, 473.

p. 65 Charlotte Brontë to W. S. Williams, September 1848. Quoted in Barker, 1998, 206–207.

p. 65 Charlotte Brontë, "Biographical Notice of Ellis and Acton Bell," 1850. Ibid., 140.

p. 66 Ibid.

p. 69 Anonymous reviewer in The Critic, 4 July 1846. Quoted in Barker, 1995, 497.

p. 69 Charlotte Brontë, "Biographical Notice," 1850. Ibid., 499.

p. 70 Charlotte Brontë to Ellen Nussey, 10 July 1846. Ibid., 504.

p. 73 Charlotte Brontë to Smith, Elder & Co., 7 August 1847. Quoted in Barker, 1998, 164.

p. 74 George Smith, A Memoir with Some Pages of Autobiography, 1902. Ibid., 165.

p. 75 G. H. Lewes, "Jane Eyre / Review," Fraser's Magazine, December 1847. Ibid., 169–170.

p. 75 William Makepeace Thackeray to W. S. Williams, 23 October 1847. Ibid., 171.

p. 76 Elizabeth Gaskell to Catherine Winkworth, 25 August 1850. Quoted in Barker, 1995, 546.

p. 76 J. G. Lockhart to a Friend, 29 December 1847. Quoted in Barker, 1998, 176.

p. 77 "Review of Wuthering Heights," The Examiner, 8 January 1848. Ibid., 177.

p. 77 Charlotte Brontë to Ellen Nussey, 11 January 1848. Ibid., 179.

p. 78 T. C. Newby to Emily Jane Brontë, 5 February 1848. Quoted in Barker, 1995, 533.

p. 79 Charlotte Brontë, Editor's Preface, Wuthering Heights, London: Smith, Elder & Co. 1850. Ibid., 534.

p. 79 Ibid., 612.

p. 80 "Review of The Tenant of Wildfell Hall," Sharpe's London Magazine, August 1848. Quoted in Barker, 1998, 194.

pp. 80–81   Charlotte Brontë to Ellen Nussey, 28 July 1848. Ibid., 201.

p. 83   Charlotte Brontë to W. S. Williams, 13 June 1849. Quoted in Gordon, 1994, 187.

pp. 84–85   Charlotte Brontë to W. S. Williams, 6 October 1848. Quoted in Barker, 1995, 568.

p. 85   Charlotte Brontë to W. S. Williams. Ibid., 576.

p. 86   Charlotte Brontë to W. S. Williams, 25 December 1848. Ibid., 578.

p. 86   Charlotte Brontë to W. S. Williams, 20 December 1848. Quoted in Barker, 1998, 216.

p. 87   Anne Brontë, "A Dreadful Darkness Closes In," 7–28 January 1849. Quoted in Barker, 1995, 582.

p. 88   Ellen Nussey, *Reminiscences* 1855–71. Quoted in Barker, 1998, 234.

p. 89   Charlotte Brontë to W. S. Williams, June 13 1849. Ibid., 238.

p. 89   Charlotte Brontë to W. S. Williams, 13 July 1849. Quoted in Barker, 1995, 597.

p. 91   Charlotte Brontë to James Taylor, 22 May 1850. Quoted in Barker, 1906, 609.

p. 92   Kathryn White, *The Brontës* (Gloucestershire, England: Sutton Publishing, Ltd., 1998), 87.

p. 93   Charlotte Brontë to Ellen Nussey. Quoted in Barker, 1995, 604.

p. 93   "Review of *Shirley,*" *Daily News,* 31 October 1849. Quoted in Barker, 1998, 247.

p. 93   Charlotte Brontë to Elizabeth Gaskell, 17 November 1849. Ibid., 250.

p. 94   Charlotte Brontë to Ellen Nussey, 4 December 1849. Ibid., 251.

p. 95   *Bradford Observer,* 28 February 1850. Quoted in Barker, 1995, 629.

p. 95   Charlotte Brontë to James Taylor, 22 May 1850. Quoted in Barker, 1998, 280.

pp. 95–96   Charlotte Brontë to Ellen Nussey, 4 December 1849. Quoted in Barker, 1995, 646.

p. 97   Charlotte Brontë, "Biographical Notice of Ellis and Acton Bell," 1850. Ibid., 655.

p. 98   Charlotte Brontë to Ellen Nussey, 23 October 1850. Quoted in Barker, 1998, 304.

p. 98   Charlotte Brontë to Ellen Nussey, 23 April 1851. Ibid., 317.

p. 98   Charlotte Brontë to Patrick Brontë, 30 May 1851. Ibid., 321.

pp. 98–99   George Smith, *A Memoir with Some Pages of Autobiography.* Ibid., 322–323.

pp. 100–101   Charlotte Brontë to George Smith, 30 October 1852. Quoted in Barker, 1995, 705.

p. 101   Charlotte Brontë to George Smith, 3 November 1852. Ibid., 705.

p. 103   Charlotte Brontë to Ellen Nussey, 15 December 1852. Ibid., 711.

pp. 103–104   Ibid., 710.

p. 104   Ibid.

p. 105   *Literary Gazette,* 5 February 1853. Quoted in Barker, 1998, 365.

p. 105   Harriet Martineau, "Review," *Daily News,* 3 February 1853. Ibid., 364.

p. 105   Charlotte Brontë to Harriet Martineau, January/February 1853. Ibid., 364.

p. 105   Charlotte Brontë to Ellen Nussey, 6 April 1853. Quoted in Barker, 1998, 369.

p. 106   Charlotte Brontë to Ellen Nussey, 16 May 1853. Ibid., 370.

p. 106   Charlotte Brontë to Ellen Nussey, 27 May 1853. Ibid., 372.

p. 106   Elizabeth Gaskell to a Friend, September 1853. Ibid., 378.

p. 107   Barker, 1995, 741.

p. 107   Charlotte Brontë to George Smith, 10 December 1853. Quoted in Barker, 1998, 381.

p. 107   Charlotte Brontë to Ellen Nussey, 28 March 1854. Quoted in Barker, 1995, 745.

p. 108   Charlotte Brontë to Ellen Nussey, 11 April 1854. Quoted in Barker, 1998, 384.

p. 110   Charlotte Brontë to Margaret Wooler, 10 July 1854. Ibid., 390.

p. 110   Charlotte Brontë to Margaret Wooler, 19 September 1854. Ibid., 393.

p. 110   Charlotte Brontë to Ellen Nussey, 20 October 1854. Quoted in Barker, 1995, 763–764.

p. 111   Charlotte Brontë to Ellen Nussey, 19 January 1855. Quoted in Barker, 1998, 396–397.

p. 112   Elizabeth Gaskell, *Life of Charlotte Brontë*. Ibid., 771.

p. 112   Arthur Nicholls to Ellen Nussey, 31 March 1855. Ibid., 399.

p. 113   Ellen Nussey to George Smith, 1 June 1860. Quoted in Barker, 1995, 773.

p. 113   Patrick Brontë to Elizabeth Gaskell, 5 April 1855. Ibid., 774.

116   Partrick Brontë to George Smith, 30 March 1857. Ibid., 798.

116   Patrick Brontë to Elizabeth Gaskell, 30 July 1857. Ibid., 803.

Selected Bibliography

Books

Alexander, Christine. *The Early Writings of Charlotte Brontë.* New York: Prometheus Books, 1983.

Barker, Juliet. *The Brontës.* London: Weidenfeld and Nicolson, 1995.

———. *The Brontës: A Life in Letters.* Woodstock and New York: The Overlook Press, 1998.

Barnard, Robert. *Emily Brontë. The British Library Writers' Lives.* London: The British Library, 2000.

Brontë, Branwell. *The Poems of Patrick Branwell Brontë,* ed. by Tom Winnifrith. Oxford: Published for the Shakespeare Head Press by Basil Blackword, 1938.

Brontë, Emily Jane. *The Complete Poems,* ed. by Janet Gezari. London: Penguin Classics, 1992.

Chitham, Edward. *A Life of Anne Brontë.* Oxford, England, and Cambridge, MA: Blackwell Publishers, 1991.

———. *A Life of Emily Brontë.* Oxford, England, and New York: Blackwell Publishers, 1987.

Davies, Stevie. *Emily Brontë: The Artist as a Free Woman*. Manchester, England: Carcanet Press Limited, 1983.

du Maurier, Daphne. *The Infernal World of Branwell Brontë*. Garden City, NY: Doubleday and Co., Inc., 1961.

Frank, Katherine. *Emily Brontë*. London: Penguin Books, 1990.

Fraser, Rebecca. *Charlotte Brontë*. London: Methuen and Crown Publishing, 1988.

Gardiner, Juliet. *The Brontës at Haworth: A Life in Letters, Diaries, and Writings*. London: Collins and Brown, Ltd., 1992.

Gaskell, Elizabeth. *The Life of Charlotte Brontë*. London: Penguin Books, 1985.

Gerin, Winifred. *Anne Brontë*. New York: Thomas Nelson and Sons, Ltd., 1959.

―――. *Branwell Brontë*. New York: Thomas Nelson and Sons, Ltd., 1961.

Gilbert, Sandra M., and Susan Gubar. *The Madwoman in the Attic*. New Haven: Yale University Press, 1984.

Gordon, Lyndall. *Charlotte Brontë: A Passionate Life*. New York and London: W. W. Norton & Co., 1994.

Hollis, Elizabeth. *Anne Brontë's Radical Vision*. Victoria, B.C.: University of Victoria, 1994.

Kinsley, Edith Ellsworth. *Pattern for Genius*. New York: E. P. Dutton, 1939.

Knapp, Bettina. *The Brontës: Branwell, Anne, Emily, Charlotte*. New York: Frederick Ungar Book, 1991.

Lane, Margaret. *The Brontë Story: A Reconsideration of Mrs. Gaskell's "Life of Charlotte Brontë."* New York: Duell, Sloan, and Pearce, 1953.

O'Byrne, Cathal. *The Gaelic Source of the Brontë Genius*. Folcroft, PA: Folcroft Library Editions, 1969.

Pool, Daniel. *What Jane Austen Ate and Charles Dickens Knew*. New York: Simon & Schuster, 1993.

Ratchford, Fannie. *The Brontë's Web of Childhood*. New York: Russell and Russell, Inc., 1964.

Sellars, Jane. *Charlotte Brontë*. London: The British Library, 1997.

White, Kathryn. *The Brontës*. Gloucestershire, England: Sutton Publishing, Ltd., 1998.

Wilks, Brian. *The Illustrated Brontës of Haworth*. New York and Oxford: Facts on File Publications, 1986.

Winnifrith, Tom. *The Brontës*. New York: Macmillan Publishing Co., Inc., 1977.

―――. *A New Life of Charlotte Brontë*. Basingstoke and London: Macmillan, 1988.

Journal Articles

Alexander, Christine. "Art and Artists in Charlotte Brontë's Juvenilia." *Brontë Society Transactions* 20, no. 4 (1991): 177–203.

Birkett, Jean K. "Sarah Garrs Newsome: An Odyssey from Haworth to the Hawkeye State." *Brontë Society Transactions* 20, no. 4 (1991): 213–216.

Carache, Marian. "Heathcliff and Catherine: No Coward Souls." *Brontë Society Transactions* 19, no. 3 (1987): 119–123.

Chitham, Edward, ed., "Mildred Christian on the Lydia Robinson Affair." *Brontë Society Transactions* 21, (1994): 71–77.

Fattorini, Victoria. "Early Nineteenth Century Cooking in Haworth." *The Brontë Society.* Shipley, England: Caxton Press,1991. (The Brontë Society and The Gaskell Society Joint Conference, 1990.)

Fraser, Rebecca. "A Strange Plant: Charlotte Brontë's Friendship with Mrs. Gaskell." *Brontë Society Transactions* 19, no. 8 (1989): 368–369.

Hannah, Barbara. "Victims of the Creative Spirit: A Contribution to the Psychology of the Brontës from the Jungian Point of View." The Guild of Pastoral Psychology (n.d.).

Sellars, Jane. "Art and the Artist as Heroine in the Novels of Charlotte, Emily and Anne Brontë." *Brontë Society Transactions* 20, no. 2 (1990): 57–76.

Magazine Articles

Bailey, Ben. "Charlotte Brontë on Honeymoon." *Ireland of the Welcomes* 41, no. 5 (September/October 1992): 32–36.

———. "Brontë Country: A Landscape of Imagination." *Victoria Magazine* 3, no. 2, (April 1989): 52–59, 136.

Watson, Bruce. "For a While, the Luddites Had a Smashing Success." *Smithsonian.* (April 1993): 140–154.

Internet

The Bronte Birthplace
<http://www.brontebirthplace.org.uk>
Bronte Parsonage Museum
<http://www.brontë.org.uk>

Novels by the Brontës

Brontë, Anne. *Agnes Grey*. London: T. C. Newby, December 1847.
———. *The Tenant of Wildfell Hall*. London: T. C. Newby, June 1848.

Brontë, Charlotte. *Jane Eyre*. London: Smith, Elder & Co., October 1847.
———. *Shirley*. London: Smith, Elder & Co., October 1849.
———. *Villette*. London: Smith, Elder & Co., January 1853.
———. *The Professor*. London: Smith, Elder & Co., 1857.
———. "Emma" (unfinished novel). Published by Smith, Elder & Co., London, as "The Last Sketch" in *Cornhill Magazine,* 1860.

Brontë, Emily. *Wuthering Heights*. London: T. C. Newby, December 1847.

Index

Photo Acknowledgments

Photographs and artwork have been reproduced with the permission of: © Brian Seed, Courtesy of the Brontë Society, pp. 2, 14, 17, 18, 30, 31, 37, 47, 59, 68, 82; © Brian Seed, pp. 6-7, 22, 32, 52, 62, 88, 94; © Brown Brothers, pp. 10, 64; © Hulton|Archive/Getty Images, pp. 16, 24, 45, 73, 77, 90; © The Brontë Society, pp. 20, 26, 39, 78, 84, 109; © Mary Evans Picture Library, pp. 35, 49, 74, 92, 96, 100, 102, 112; © National Portrait Gallery, London, p. 36; © Brian Seed, Courtesy of the R.C. Holroyd Family of Stone Gappe Hall, p. 42; © Brian Seed, Courtesy of Rene Pechere, p. 55; © Nina Barton Owens, Courtesy of the Author, p. 128.

Front cover © National Portrait Gallery, London. Front and back cover © Brian Seed.

Acknowledgments

I thank Richard, my son, and Yvonne, my daughter-in-law, for traveling with me twice to Haworth, England, to visit the Brontë Parsonage Museum and for our walk on the moors. I also thank *British Heritage* magazine and the *Christian Science Monitor* for publishing my Brontë articles in the 1990s. For my research, I am in debt to Kathryn White and later Ann Dinsdale, both of the Brontë Parsonage Museum; The British Library and The British Museum; the University of California, San Diego, Library; and the Huntington Library in Pasadena. I thank Nina Barton Owens, for taking my author photo for this book. Finally my appreciation to Sara Saetre and Marcia Marshall, editors at Lerner Publishing Group, for working with me on my manuscript. And I thank and acknowledge the spirits of the Brontës.

Karen Smith Kenyon

About the Author

Karen Smith Kenyon first visited the Brontë Parsonage Museum in Haworth, West Yorkshire, England, in 1992 and again in 1994. These visits to the home of the Brontës gave birth to research which led to major articles in *British Heritage* magazine and the *Christian Science Monitor* and grew into this young adult biography.

Ms. Kenyon researched extensively, using the University of California, San Diego collection of Brontë biographies, as well as *The Brontë Society Transactions,* and the San Diego Public Library. She was granted permission to read original copies of Charlotte Brontë's letters at the Huntington Library in San Marino, California. She also visited the British Museum and the British Library in London, where she saw original manuscripts and artifacts. In addition, she consulted frequently by mail with Kathryn White and Ann Dinsdale of the Brontë Parsonage Museum.

Ms. Kenyon was born in Guthrie, Oklahoma, and grew up there and in Sacramento, California. Her mother was a pianist, and music was a great influence on her early life.

Her writing career began in 1973 with "A Young Mother's Story" in *Redbook* magazine. She then went on to earn a Master of Arts degree in English with an emphasis in creative writing, as she continued writing articles, poetry, and essays. A book, *Sunshower,* about the untimely death of her husband, was published by G. P. Putnam's Sons in 1981 and soon after she began teaching college writing courses.